## About the Author

A law dean for ten years, the author also served as President of the Philippine Association of Law Schools and Chairman of the Board of Trustees of the Pamantasan ng Lungsod ng Maynila. He was the Chief Government Corporate Counsel of former President Gloria Arroyo and Chairman of the Social Security Commission under President Rodrigo Duterte. He was involved in controversial cases like the impeachment of former President Joseph Estrada and a crucial presidential disqualification case in the 2016 elections. His newspaper column *'Magpayo Nga Kayo'*, or 'Brainstorming with the people', was a finalist in the 2004 Catholic Mass Media Awards (often referred to locally as CMMA).

That a Man Dies Ignorant When
He Has Capacity for Knowledge,
is A Tragedy

**Amado D. Valdez**

That a Man Dies Ignorant When
He Has Capacity for Knowledge,
is A Tragedy

Olympia Publishers
*London*

**www.olympiapublishers.com**
OLYMPIA PAPERBACK EDITION

A CIP catalogue record for this title is
available from the British Library.

ISBN: 978-1-80074-428-8

Names and characters, other than those who are part of Philippine
history, are the author's imagination of composite traits of several
persons and events. Any resemblance to actual persons, living or
dead is purely coincidental.

First Published in 2023

Olympia Publishers
Tallis House
2 Tallis Street
London
EC4Y 0AB

Printed in Great Britain

# Dedication

To my late parents, Melquiades and Feliciana and my wife, Nellie.

# Acknowledgements

My deepest gratitude to my wife, Nellie, whose encouragement never faded. To former Presidents Joseph 'Erap' Estrada, Gloria Macapagal-Arroyo, and President Rodrigo R. Duterte for their trust and friendship. To the late Senator Heherson 'Sonny' Alvarez and wife Cecile who allowed me to be part of their journey. To former Speaker, Jose de Venecia Jr. and wife, Gina de Venecia for their fellowship, and former Vice President Jejomar Binay for his camaraderie.

To the inspirations of my life: Melquiades Marcus II and Aiza Katrina, Amadeus Aurelius and Wendy, Jason Roland and Elizabeth who made my life complete by giving me loving grandchildren: Summer Rose, Amado Vittorio II, Arya, Zachariah Deen and Aurora Katerina.

EVERY EVIL IS IGNORANCE, EVERY GOOD IS WISDOM
— SOCRATES —

# Contents

# INTRODUCTION

Amado D. Valdez is one of the country's most distinguished lawyers and public intellectuals. As former dean of the University of the East College of Law, his voice is often sought to clarify discordant views on the Constitution. As a civic and political activist (he was formerly the Bureau Director of Legal Agrarian Assistance) he organised the 'Barefoot Lawyers Program' which unclogged the dockets of the Ministry of Agrarian Reform. As Director of the Integrated Bar of the Philippines' (IBP) Legal Aid Program, he initiated projects to improve the country's justice system, the protection of abused women and children, the training of paralegals, the decongestion of jails, among others. As Chairman of the Philippine's Social Security Commission, he increased the pension of retirees in the private sector.

Now, as he breaches the peak of a productive and meaningful career, he took time out to write this elegant and revealing autobiography. It reads like a novel of memory. It was Graham Greene who once said that the best material for any writer are the memories of his boyhood; they are the most lasting and vivid. Valdez writes lovingly of his boyhood in a small Ilokano town. His description of his rural background is reminiscent of Manuel Arguilla's [1] *The Scent of the Earth*, the

---

[1] An Ilocano writer in English who authored a book about nature and its landscape.

grandeur of the landscape, the fields. He also paints his characters with fidelity; they seem almost real, his father most of all, who was a minister of the Iglesia Ni Cristo[2]. Valdez dedicates this book to him and to his mother—the two great influences in his life. His father, a disciplinarian, was rather rigid in raising a family.

He ran away from his hometown to live in Manila, where soon enough, he underwent his first traumatic experience in a café close to the school where he went. He was beaten up and when he regained consciousness, he was in a hospital.

This autobiography could be titled *The Education of Amado D. Valdez* because even when he was recuperating, he recalled the incidents in his boyhood wherein basic questions on life and faith were already bothering him. There, he pondered what he had done, the learning, maturing process had begun.

In his pain, he recognises the necessity of having to strive. He was sixteen years old.

In school, he immersed himself in the study of history and philosophy and he understood how philosophy can explain life. This autobiography is thus a personal introduction to Western philosophy too as it applies to life.

Amado D. Valdez is particularly fond of Socrates who influenced him in his career. The autobiography reads like a picaresque novel as he moves from one particular region of the country to another. Meanwhile, he never loses his sense of observation of the land and the people, especially those in the provinces.

He had of course many disappointments. When his father

---

[2] a Philippine indigenous Christian sect.

died, for instance, the church which his father served so long and well, did not take care of his burial[3]. That did not diminish his spirituality.

All over this autobiography are snatches of political insights. As an activist, the author often moved in the ozone regions of society; he had close relationships with many national leaders. He has been very candid in his views about them and on government as he was often consulted by them. He is deeply aware of this country's problems, particularly the moral decay and how it has gone down; he grew up with the common people and learnt from them, and as a lawyer helped them.

Make no mistake—this autobiography is a lucid commentary as well on Philippine history in the last century. In telling his story, Valdez also illustrates what one man — motivated and sincere — can do for his country or any man for the country he loves. The last portion of this book is an outline of Philippine politics, particularly the presidency, some of the goings-on in the corridors of power are exposed for the first time.

Amado D. Valdez concludes his beautiful autobiography with a lament of what was not done. This is a cue for us to think and do what must be done.

**F. SIONIL JOSE**
National Artist for Literature
2001 — Philippines

---

[3] Please see details in Chapter 14 — "My Father Finally Smiled".

# FOREWORD

This memoir tackles the dilemma of a young boy who broke the chain of ignorance at the price of disobeying his father, significantly depriving himself of the latter's spiritual wisdom and guidance.

But it was worth the risk. His life's trajectory finds itself intersecting with the downfall of a president, the fruitful but unappreciated stint of his successor and the election to power of a political maverick who rewrote the political game in his country, the Philippines.

Living alone in Manila after his escape from home in 1961, he found the company of young students similarly situated. Together, they examined their personal lives and their country's fate and struggled to break the age-old chains binding them to poverty, hopelessness, dependency and lack of self-esteem.

Meeting at the student canteens in the university belt at the centre of the City of Manila in the 1960s, they exchanged thoughts, individual biases and preferences. The informal jousts plucked them from darkness to a recognition of the need for education, independence of will and rationality against the commanding and controlling influence of religion and superstition, foreign intervention, elitism, and dominance of the privileged class.

It is a story of the shared struggle of the sons of labourers, farmers and ordinary folks from the countryside to educate themselves, both culturally and intellectually.

Their days in the canteen coincided with the Cuban Missile Crisis pushing the world to the brink of destruction, and the cultural revolution in China, the most populous country in the world, in upheaval. The consequences of these events made their vision for their country more realistic to accommodate the reality of geopolitics.

The philosophy and practical thought they developed prepared them for leadership, whether in business, politics, or the academe. Their core beliefs were formulated and developed together in their regular meetings in their own Ziatna Moruna, their 1960s version of those held at the cafe in Belgrade, that nursed the idea which brought about the disintegration of the old European empires in the aftermath of World War I.

The narrative starts with the author's escape from his home which brought him to a near-death situation in a hospital. He confronted his own guilt by further keeping distance from his father, but his independent course made him realise that an unexamined life is not worth living, that doing good for its own sake and not for a heavenly reward has its own delight, that the best education comes from experience, and that spirituality and religious belief are personal and not hereditary. It finally ends with the consequences of his and his colleagues' triumph over the evil of ignorance.

By and large, it explains the present Filipino zeitgeist [4] and mirrors third world countries' aspirations to pursue their own destiny for the rest of the world to understand.

---

[4] General intellectual, moral and cultural climate of an era.

By design, the author defines the universal aspiration of man regardless of race, gender, nationality and economic circumstances to be free in his thoughts and proposes a new belief system of a sublime power that is personal to man as he feels its presence and existence in his life, without the representation, dependence or agency of organised religion and merchants of hope for the afterlife.

Hopefully, by breaking the chain of ignorance, this memoir helps establish the norm of spiritual and secular life in the future!

# PROLOGUE

Always compliant and doted upon by my father, I committed a horrible act. Yet it was not a mindless or childish display of defiance. What made it unprecedented was that it was unexpected even to a father deeply scarred by his own experience of youthful exuberance.

Admittedly, to begin a long but single journey in life, it would be a miscalculation to start with the wrong foot. It is no wonder that many had expected a hard life for this young lad.

Initially, I paid a heavy price. With time, however, I discovered, in reality I was paying for experiences whose importance would only be known later in life much like a French Champagne which got better with the passing years, until finally popped open as a reward to celebrate the winning of a race or a game.

It is exactly as Ralph Waldo Emerson had explained:

"The years teach much which the days never knew."

In time, I learnt about discipline, self-restraint and tolerance. Through life's ups and downs I gathered a treasure trove of knowledge.

\*

When my father objected to my plan to study in Manila, I turned to prayers!

I did not pray to an old venerable man with a white beard, who could order the wind to stop or the stars to turn their light off or show up in a bush of fire. My idea of God is not in that context of social consciousness but a private and personal experience of a higher presence beyond any possible imagination.

At sixteen years old, I was already a maverick.

To my dismay, God took my father's side and punished me immediately for my impertinence. Two months after my escape from home under the cover of darkness, I found myself in a hospital bed, beaten and unconscious.

Instead of giving up, I viewed my close call with death positively and the start of my education on how to function in this world. It meant abandoning old beliefs and the first to go was my father's diktat, which is the pursuit and expectation of an afterlife as the motivating force of one's conduct.

There is delight in doing good for its own sake. This relieved me from the burden of keeping score with that fanatical quest to be in heaven. Life became less burdensome. I merely simplified it by removing the 'O' from good, then you are in God's page. It is a simple arithmetic and not a riddle hidden in enigmas and puzzles and metaphors that cannot be understood. It does not require rituals like lighting candles, attending church, showing piety, penance and self-flagellation. Nor does it depend upon offerings to build cathedrals to house 'God' who promises in return a mansion for you to stay in rebirth after you die.

This thinking entailed self-doubt at first because it ran against the established way of doing things. To a young kid who disobeys his father or doing away with his belief system is likely to result in a sort of paranoia, a voice telling him that he was damned, a self-fulfilling failure.

Fortunately, life is not a sprint but a marathon with turns and twists in which your free will allows for adjustments along the way. Definitely, life is not predetermined according to a script written in advance.

This is not my story alone. It is also your story, though unfolding in your own unique way; it is a tale about finding your own space in this world and how through your struggles you can discover meaning in life.

# PART ONE

# 1

# IT IS HARD, BUT A NURSE OF GOOD LADS

It may have been hours that I was unconscious but when I came to, there was dryness in the walls of my throat. I was choking and breathless. Luckily, my lungs breathed out air so strong to clear the obstruction that allowed me to inhale.

For a while, there was a sigh of relief, but the whiff of a hospital bed and the sound of moaning distressed me. Even the cry of a newborn infant did not give me hope.

I raised my hand like a cup to my mouth to discover a clot of dry blood. There was pain all over my body. My head was buzzing and heavy with a thick bandage wrapped around it. I wanted to stand but my leg was also in pain.

I heard the doctor tell the nurse on duty to keep an eye on me for the next twenty-four hours. He explained it was possible that I may have suffered a severe concussion and might have lost the ability to talk and other functions.

"What time is it? What happened?" I tested my body but could not hear my voice.

"Do you remember anything?" The nurse asked, lightly tapping my shoulders, the first expressive touch of a woman other than my mother. Her voice was soothing! My blood surged! It made me a little buoyant.

This was the first time I came so close, a foot away, to the

29

face of a young woman. The nurse who was clad in white but without the training white cap looked pleasant. I thought she was reaching out to give me a reassuring hug.

Out of all of my experiences in the hospital, I remember this experience the most because of some levity being frequently exchanged about waking up in a hospital and seeing the face of an angel.

*'Avoir la chair de poule'.*[5]

Perhaps it was wrong to feel excited but then it meant I was alive. I felt dizzy and then it was all black. The last thing I heard was the nurse frantically telling another to call for a doctor.

Another nurse was there when I woke up. She spoke my dialect and we exchanged pleasantries in Ilocano[6]. It was reassuring to feel the presence of someone familiar. They say Ilocanos, like the families in the Scottish Highlands, are very clannish as if it were a vice but this time that I am in pain and broken such kinship is a welcome relief.

In the afternoon, the police came. He inquired about the people who were at the canteen when the ruckus happened. The police said something about a fraternity initiation.

Fraternity affairs are a big thing in school especially initiations which could be grounds for expulsion.

Now it all seemed very clear. The previous night I was with a group of six students seated around a big round table in a canteen in the vicinity of the school talking about anything that caught our fancy. One of them was a Hot Head who I recall just stormed out of his seat fuming before the assault.

---

[5] Goose bumps in French.
[6] A Filipino dialect in the north.

The investigating policeman was kind enough not to press his interview. I heard him say my statement would not be considered in articulo mortis[7] anyway. Whatever it was that the policeman was saying, the body language of the doctor who was checking on me at the same time contributed to the policeman's backtracking to my great relief.

About six p.m., an unlikely visitor arrived. His voice is unmistakable. Gone was the long hair he'd worn when I first met him in the passenger bus coming to the city from the province two months back.

"Lakay,"[8] he said, "thank you for the bananas." I smiled. He attracts curiosity with the way he talks and moves. He is not easily stereotyped which made him distinguishable, yet unmistakably with a common air!

"You were in good company at the wrong time!" he said with a hint that he had been watching me ever since I arrived in the city.

"One of the students was drunk. He was particularly mad at you for something you may have done or something you represent which unfortunately he is not. He hit you on the head," he told me.

He did not pause, clearly not wanting his flow of thought to be interrupted. Anyhow, I was not really in any condition to exchange words. As a result, I felt like I was just a part of his imagined audience.

As he spoke, I recalled the last time I saw Manny. He was handcuffed and sitting in a police jeep.

---

[7] At the point of death
[8] Literally, old man but in practice is used endearingly to refer to a guy from the same region.

"Your friend gets his news here as a radio reporter," the nurse volunteered.

News flies and this kind of news is good or bad. There is relief that succour from my parents is not far behind but then I am damned.

I disobeyed my father when I was sixteen years old by leaving home and the only way to redeem myself was to go back to him fulfilled with a college degree. However, the scenario that is quickly shaping up is different. I will be thrown out of the university and almost surely guaranteed a future of scrubbing floors or cleaning streets. I feel as though I am falling down from a devastating blow and need to clinch or hold on to the ropes. The best option is to go back to my father's home, I think.

\*

When I arrived in the city in 1962, I enrolled in a university near my boarding house. But it was outside the university, in an informal canteen, where a parallel learning was underway. Better than the four walls of our liberal arts school, this canteen was a workshop of ideas that gave me a better appreciation, a world view, a broader perspective of day-to-day issues.

This makeshift school was free to those willing to learn and there are no admission tests, but the final reckoning lies in the future. It exacts a toll—your contribution to collective wisdom and enlightenment on a potpourri of things. You are embarrassed there, admired, or like me, you sustain a wound on the head, a cracked bone, and land in a hospital unconscious. Still, it was a small price, a bargain for what you received in return as you will see.

I owe it to a bespectacled student who was my classmate in a philosophy class in finding such a gem of a school. He was a fellow Ilocano from Tarlac[9] province, also a pre-law student with a journalism major. He did not become a lawyer but a few years after graduation from college he wrote a regular column — 'Through a Dark Glass' — making sense of current events as we did in our jousts at the canteen. The profession he chose required him to burn the midnight oil dry prematurely, but he bequeathed me with the light of understanding that lasts a lifetime.

"An unexamined life is not worth living," his soft voice opening a chest of knowledge like a thunderbolt.

I regarded him with great awe. Perhaps the reason for my high esteem is he described what I had wanted all along when I escaped from my father's home. Such a profound thought was like a fire that ignited the urge to examine my personal experiences with my inner sense and not through the eyes of my father and the prism fixed by his environment made up of like-minded but deeply spiritual people.

"No, that is not original, that is Socrates!" he clarified.

The beauty and the simplicity of Socrates drew me into the esoteric world of my newfound friend. After the evening class, we dropped by this small canteen. It was full of students debating furiously on different issues better than a usual classroom. They talked about philosophy, politics, religion — the latter sparingly as it was divisive — government and smorgasbord of issues. I was light years away from their erudition, but I knew I could catch up. All I needed to do is

---

[9] A province in Central Luzon.

listen to them, I told myself.

The canteen was located within what is called the university belt. This area with a circumference of about a thousand hectares consists of clusters of universities in the centre of the City of Manila. It is bound on the northeast by the University of Santo Tomas, [10] a Catholic University established by the Dominicans in 1611, predating the establishment of Harvard University in the United States by twenty-five years; on the south by De la Salle University and the old campus of the University of the Philippines, the country's premier state university. By the Pasig River is the Malacañang Palace which is the official residence of the President of the Philippines and the centre of power. Farther on to the west is the sprawling Rizal Park from where you can watch the best sunset across Manila Bay on the horizon. But the northwest was bordered by the sprawling Chinatown, the centre of trade during that time.

Our university belt is reminiscent of the Ringstrasse, [11] with its cluster of monumental buildings in Vienna, Austria, although it is a poor cousin. While it lacked the Austrian pomposity, the university belt nonetheless spawned informal centres which included our small canteen as a meeting place of students eager to learn more but some use it as a pulpit to explore their dreamy ideas.

"This is our Zlatna Moruna," my friend told me.

By my blank expression, he felt he had to explain.

Zlatna Moruna is a café in Belgrade where the idea to assassinate Austrian Archduke Franz Ferdinand was hatched

---

[10] Oldest university in Asia and the Philippines.
[11] Circular grand boulevard.

by a band of young terrorists that brought the downfall of the old empires of Europe and from the debris rose many new and free nations including Yugoslavia. His death was used by the Austro-Hungarian Empire to attack Serbia and precipitated World War I. These common criminals, as they were thought of then, are now the patriots of their country. History was kind to them in the aftermath of World War I.

The radical nationalists of Zlatna Moruna Café took just two months to ignite the fire that burned to the ground the old Europe with the downfall of the Austro-Hungarian Empire and Tsarist Russia as compared to the years and decade for our ideas in the canteen to hold sway. This made me reflect about the universality of the youth's mind and common aspiration of his soul.

In present-day Manila, the small canteens in the university belt have been replaced by Western-inspired cafes, foremost of which is the Starbucks which has become ubiquitous all over the world. I would bet that the founder of Starbucks was inspired by Café Grinsted in Ringstrasse in the early 20th century which allowed customers to stay in the café as long as he made a single purchase of a cup of coffee.

The banter among students now in this modern-day Café Grinsted could be more subdued but the atmosphere of passion in exchanging thoughts has not changed. If there is the contrast between then and now, these are the tablets and laptops hooked to the internet, replacing the small pocketbooks and notebooks of my time. Googling is the quick way to knowledge and information among students nowadays instead of recall, original thoughts and native intelligence that characterised our exchanges in our small canteens. I hope that this unassisted way of thought process is not lost by the new generation.

Then and now, if you want to feel the cravings of the youth, the zeitgeist of the times, just stay a week in a student canteen.

*

Once in the canteen, the exchange among the students who were there earlier than us was spirited, not lacking the confidence of my friend in quoting the expressed thoughts of Socrates. It did not escape me, however, that one of them was deliberate and conscious of displaying his newfound knowledge and not to illuminate.

It is this discomfiture that caused me to say in a tone more than a whisper how ignorant I was in comparison. My writer friend made me feel good.

"Ignorance is the beginning of wisdom," he assured me. "But to stay ignorant is evil. The only good is knowledge," he continued.

"Socrates," he said.

He told me that Socrates is one of a trio — Plato, and Aristotle being the other two — all Greeks, who influenced the thought of Western civilisation. They are called classical philosophers as distinguished from the natural philosophers who came before them, the most prominent of whom was Democritus.

Democritus was Socrates' contemporary and in fact, died after the latter but his ideas belonged to the pre-Socratic. Democritus and the other natural philosophers believed that nothing comes from nothing, and the world is built from tiny invisible blocks. Democritus claimed that even the soul is made of special, smooth, round atoms that are part of the brain and flows to all directions when the brain disintegrates. This thought was called the atom theory which manifested later in modern times, the seed of the science that fuelled the leap of civilisation.

Socrates and the other classical philosophers talked about happiness, ethics, power, or anything that animates from within which became the seed of the ideas of democracy, humanism, and liberalism.

The Socratic tradition, he continued, gave us free thought while Democritus' tiny blocks gave us the computer. When the idea of the first went wild, the world caught the fire of totalitarianism and communism, while the second gave us the atomic bomb and the weapons of mass destruction. Both planted seeds that grew into trees of knowledge with fruits both sweet and bitter to mankind.

I remember my history teacher in our community college raising a question that had been originally asked by Amerigo Vespucci in 1502, the first European to discover America, in his report on the new world, why the natives made war upon each other,

"...considering that they held no private property or sovereignty of empire and kingdoms and did not know any such thing as lust for possession, that is, pillaging or a desire to rule, which appear to me to be the causes of wars and of disorderly act. When we requested them to state the cause they did not know how to give any other cause than that this curse upon them began in ancient times and they sought to avenge the deaths of their forefathers."[12]

---

[12] P.81 EYEWITNESS TO HISTORY, Edited by John Carey.

To think that the idea of Socrates had a heuristic connection to my scant knowledge of Amerigo Vespucci's insight of the native Americans, gave me a new way to build knowledge by mixing one idea with another of similar or different import. Their chemistry results in clarity or understanding of a new situation. A seed sown in a curious mind would grow to displace one's ignorance.

The realisation tuned me to absorb like a sponge a share of my friend's accumulated wisdom.

He added:

"The natural philosophers and the classical ones in succession began explaining the world based on reason and observation, a departure from the sets of religious myths handed down generation after generation before them. Together, these philosophers articulated man's sense of wonder: what we are made of, how everything works, why are we here, and where are we going?

"The sense of wonder was lost during the Middle Ages when the Catholic Church took over the will and mind of Europe with their inquisition. Then religion explaining the world based on myth came back again. Today, the religious debate is all about which version of the myth is the truth."

He gave me an introduction to Western thought, beginning with the ancients who wondered about fire and sound, then came Greeks' use of reason and logic to interpret what the senses perceived and afterwards looking inward, for that deeper need of a man, like want and happiness.

I was spellbound.

He asked me the question: "If all religion now is a myth, is not the debate on a true religion a futile exercise?"

It was a key question that jumpstarted my scrutiny of

religion, belief in God, creation, salvation, and the afterlife. What is the mystery of the unseen? These were the seminal questions that turned out to change my trajectory from my father's beliefs.

Back to Socrates, he was described as being bald and pot-bellied. I was amused by the similarity of appearance with Tata Abon, a man from back home whom I consider a sort of philosopher. [13] Another student added the trivia that Socrates' head was like a porter. If this is the guy that influenced all these starry-eyed students, my Tata Abon, a figure in my childhood, does not pale in comparison. I was beginning to gather my voice.

While Tata Abon attracted my lone attention, Socrates had brought around him young boys whom he confronted with a series of questions about what they meant in the things they say. This rigorous style of questioning became known as the Socratic Method.[14]

Some groups during Socrates' time were irritated by the critical way Socrates disturbed the accepted mindset and their fear that he was corrupting the minds of the youth. The Athenians were too intolerant that they made a crime out of the 'corruption of the young', 'neglect of the gods' and 'not believing in the accepted gods.' He was convicted in the first known injustice against the right of thought, belief, and speech.

When Socrates was awaiting his execution, his friends plotted to spring him out from prison to freedom and instead

---

[13] Informal version of father

[14] A form of cooperative argumentative dialogue between individuals based on asking and answering questions to stimulate critical thinking and to draw out ideas and underlying presuppositions.

of taking advantage of the time to make the flight, Socrates found time to leisurely question their motives and to prove the correctness of the course of action to be taken. In the end, they were not able to prevail over him to escape and so he took the poison as a manner of his execution.

One of the students quipped: "Socrates was the first casualty of his method".

The talk took a turn to the hilarious which later turned into the worst, a rather natural development in that setting.

I said that Tata Abon was far superior to Socrates on the philosophy of married life. Tata Abon kept the love of Nana[15] Ingga everlasting and always with passion the way I saw them interact. Socrates neglected his wife and children. Nana Ingga always welcomed Tata Abon back to her home, but Socrates was hardly missed by his wife and children.

I asked my new friends, "Who is better, Tata Abon or Socrates?"

This question led to my sort of baptism before the group. The serious and showy guy who caught my attention when I arrived threw the water in his glass at my face.

"That was just a question; I think it is relevant!" A cool-headed student doused him with his calm remark.

"But he is making a joke at the expense of the greatest philosopher of his time or perhaps of all ages", Mr Hot Head said.

"And who is this Tata Abon, your philosopher?" he further asked.

I nearly choked with a little smile on my face. They took it that I had let the insult of the thrown glass of water pass. The

---

[15] Nana is the informal form of mother.

truth is I was in a dilemma whether to tell them that Tata Abon was not a philosopher but a janitor. Mr Hot Head may just throw the sink at me.

When all was back to normal, I said: "Should we not be guided by a certain philosophy of marriage?", while wiping my face with a napkin. Too much of Socrates had brought the students to the cloud. They needed a question to bring them down to earth. That was all I could manage to say.

Mr Hot Head stood from his seat, went around to my back and gently pressed my shoulders. That, to me, was enough for an apology.

They ignored my question and as a newcomer, that was a blow to my self-esteem more than the water thrown at me. But I realised my question was premature. They were not done with Socrates yet.

"Do not misjudge Socrates", Mr Hot Head began. "Xanthippe, Socrates' wife loved him as much. He was respected by his disciples; they liked his company at the table and admired his modesty."

In that sense, I commented that Socrates did not only think but lived the life of a wise man. I recalled my father telling me that wisdom is knowing how to live well and that includes a good relationship with your fellow human beings. If these new friends have their philosophers, I have Job, the Proverbs, the Ecclesiastes, the wisdom books of the Bible. This puts me on par with them.

Then he sounded pedantic. "'Gnothi seauton' — know thyself! It is the beginning of Socrates' philosophy. Socrates described it clearly when he said, "I know one thing, and that is that I know nothing."

After a lull, another clarified the phrase to him in

particular, that Socrates feigned ignorance to expose what little a person knows. It was called the Socratic irony.[16]

I was not given to playing possum but being face to face with a poseur, it was easy to appear attentive while my mind was saying, *this guy is more bark than bite by not deeply understanding Socrates.*

He may have read my mind.

"Let us hear from Tata Abon," his look was more a challenge than genuinely expecting I would oblige.

I looked at my friend, Mr Glasses, and then to Mr Cool. They were smiling. It looks like Mr Hot Head was serious. He finished his third bottle of San Miguel beer. His voice became slurred and there is no doubt that he was drunk. I saw in him my old friend Putin. That encouraged me.

"Who is your philosopher?" he asked.

"He was a carpenter," I said. They threw a quizzical gaze at me as if asking whether I was serious, or this was another joke. My self-esteem was back.

"He did not speak much, and he taught us, his apprentice, with his hands," I said softly. "By example!" I added.

I continued: "By cutting lumber into its proper sizes, we learnt how to avoid waste or to economise. The repeated motions of pushing and pulling the plane on the surface of the wood to make it fine, developed patience, concentration, and dedication. Driving the nail into the delicate furniture in the making meant accuracy and self-control; collecting the tools and keeping them in one place to be easily accessible when needed is orderliness. Sharpening the blades of the saw and

---

[16] When you pretend to be ignorant to expose the ignorance or inconsistency of another.

plane is not only preparedness but an act of foresight as well."

They fell silent, spellbound by my observations, including Mr Hot Head.

"Whether the furniture we made at the end of the week was a small cabinet or a picture frame, or a small desk, we discovered satisfaction from doing the work ourselves. After seeing the raw lumber transformed into a beautiful piece of furniture through the process of cutting and fitting the pieces together into the intended symmetry, we appreciated beauty as well as creation."

"Where is this carpenter?" Mr Hot Head asked.

"He died on the cross!" said Mr Glasses.

He died early but I will never forget his intellectual mien in a frail body. I mourned him silently at that time, but he deserved a public eulogy that came many years later.

Everyone laughed at Mr Hot Head who was the last to comprehend.

"Bullshit!" shouted Mr Hot Head.

*

Mr Hot Head always reminded me of the bear in Jean de La Fontaine's story about an animal and a gardener who were both lonely and bored of long hours doing the same things. The gardener rested from cultivating fruit trees and flowers to look for a friend. At the same time, the bear longed as well for someone to talk to and left his mountain lair. They met and agreed to visit each other and from then on, they became friends. The bear was fond of catching flies and when he visited the gardener, the animal found a fly perched on the nose of the sleeping gardener. The fly was elusive, and this made the animal more obsessed. Instead of a swatter that failed to catch the fly, the animal hurled a paving stone as hard as he could to crush the fly. The 'marksmanship' was excellent but the thinking was not so good—he made a corpse of his friend, the gardener.

Thus, Jean de La Fontaine [17], a 17th-century French fabulist joined my repertoire of teachers who began with Aesop[18] at the knee of my first teacher, my mother. It was De la Fontaine who woke me up from naivete with his wise remark that the world is full of foolish men. To me, fables were more a living tool for quick learning in life than the discourses of Socrates or Plato.

*

Meanwhile, Mr Hot Head realised how much of life he failed to understand notwithstanding his mastery of Socrates and Plato. He was embarrassed when the rest of the group was laughing at him. I could not even force a smile as I sensed danger judging from the daggers in his eyes.

I could still feel the wet from the glass of water he had earlier thrown at me. And then he cursed menacingly and left.

Later, I found myself broken in a hospital bed.

*

The night seemed infinite in the hospital since the light of the morning and afternoon sun are kept away by the stained-glass

---

[17] French famous fabulist
[18] Greek fabulist and a storyteller.

windows. The clock on the wall suddenly stopped but time neither slows down nor accelerates itself. Time can only stretch the space so all the troubles in one's life cannot clog one's mind and allow a reasonable pace to ponder the next move.

I wanted an update of my case and my anticipation of my classmates' visit made me look at the doorway every now and then, but I was disappointed.

I looked through the hospital window to absorb Manila for the last time. The province may still be a better option as my father thought it was. My curiosity about the city was crowded out by a yearning for a secure and comfortable home in the province.

I closed my eyes to realise that my escape was not getting any traction.

'How true it is that nothing is sweeter than home and kindred!'

I remember reading those words in Homer's *Odyssey* and now it is coming back as an enchanting whisper.

Another voice from the same epic is describing my experience as, "It is rough, but a nurse of good lads!"

Should I choose the sweet part or the roughness of life away from home?

I am in a dilemma.

Momentarily, I realised that the trip to the hospital ward had shattered my youthful dreams. In this lap, my father scored a telling point without firing a single shot.

*

My friends came in the evening in full force, but one was

conspicuously missing.

"He left the following day after the incident," the coolest of my friends volunteered.

"We came from the dean's office today and everything has been ironed out. He will be expelled but there will be a hearing to give him a chance to explain himself."

"How about the police?" I asked.

"It is your decision," he remarked without any hint of encouragement or making an attempt to talk me out of filing any complaint.

"I have no intention to file a case," I said.

I remember Mr Hot Head and our exchange of words was spontaneous to preclude any malice to invite his aggression. I particularly liked what he shared about Socrates when he was given a cup of hemlock[19]: that pain and pleasure fastened together by God, "if the man pursues the one and captures it, he is generally obliged to take the other also, as if the two were joined together in one head." It is pleasant enough to learn such wisdom, to entomb a gratitude in my heart, the pain inflicted by his being wayward notwithstanding. Pleasure and pain, twins indeed.

I blamed the alcoholic spirits instead.

My friends looked at each other and I could sense a feeling of collective relief. I felt a certain bridge built between us which would last a lifetime.

Then somebody remarked that I should not worry about the hospital bill.

"It is already settled. We have some cash left for you", Mr Cool put it in my hands.

---

[19] Poison tea.

"We met your brother Manny at the lobby. He is in a hurry for an assignment in the province. He left this envelope for you."

When I opened it, the envelope contained a hundred pesos. I was moved by Manny's charity and to avoid betraying my sentiments, I amused myself by imagining him contrite when he nearly ate all the fruits I had on the bus. It brought me great relief because I had nothing, not even a single cent. I reminded myself of my mother's story about everyone having a guardian angel!

The hospital lights went out, a cue for my friends to leave. They offered kind words but were careful not to praise me to the skies. Their presence was stimulating and comforting but when I was alone again, I let my tears fall realising what I had become in the last few days and the genuine friendship I had earned. The repressed emotions finally released and made me feel better.

Finally, the hospital ward did not reek any more and the white uniforms moving about the ward made me feel bullish again.

Momentarily before I lost consciousness, I willed my life's sail close to the wind.

# 2
# A CHILD'S PLAY

My initial sentient experience was a fragment of light framed by an open window illuminating two people in an animated huddle. Their voices were hushed as if they were respectful of the silence and unmindful of the darkness outside where I was seated. Such ambience made me look into the light coming from the house which turned out to be a positive thing to do.

The light made me unafraid of the dark around me.

I was calm even in a night that is pitch-black. This courage, a defiance of the dark or any vapid feeling boded well in every aspect of life I was involved with in the years ahead. So that, in one event after the other, whether good or bad, the experience would make me stronger and resilient like the Rose of Jericho, [20] a desert plant whose branches fold inwards to form a ball.

\*

In junior high school, for example, part of my scouting experience included sleeping overnight over tombs at a cemetery during Halloween. To overcome our fear, the

---

[20] The small grey plant curls its branches and seedpods inward in the dry season, forming a ball that opens only when moistened.

scoutmaster would assign one boy scout to a single tomb at ten metres apart from each other. I had my apprehension, but it was not fear from being alone on a tomb in a dark night but from snakes or other kinds of crawling dangers.

When I mentioned my concern about the snakes to our scoutmaster, he told me that snakes are more afraid of people than us of them. Rat snakes slither away when they hear a rustling noise, but a cobra is steadier and ready to bite to defend himself. After determining you are not threat to him, he will leave.

Among human beings, he continued, the rat snakes are more dangerous than the cobras. The rat snake kills you by stabbing you in the back. This last part was obviously a non sequitur[21] and alerted me that I was in the middle of a silent war when the scoutmaster, daggers in his eyes, looked at my classmate who was obviously distressed. Of the many tombs available for every scout, he assigned a fresh tomb in which a corpse had just been interred to this classmate. Later, when the scoutmaster was gone, I discovered the cause of the animosity. My classmate told me a shocking secret. He saw our scoutmaster kissing a teenage sister of our Indian classmate. It was a lesson to me about the kind of deadly information one would rather avoid knowing.

Back in the hospital I broke into a wry smile recalling that early introduction to gossip and how at the time it was just burlesque, having no label or name, but in contemporary times it was no longer taken lightly and was even given a name:

---

[21] A conclusion or reply that does not follow logically from the previous statement.

paedophilia. [22] Many years would pass before I met that classmate again; he updated me of our disciplinarian scoutmaster. He said that in his old age our scoutmaster became a snake collector and had died after one of his rat snakes bit him. I thought that he waited for this ill-fate to give vent to his feelings against our scoutmaster. There are people who could hold a grudge forever and forget to move on in life. When he introduced to me his son, I changed my mind. His son was half-Indian and the mother was our Indian classmate's sister.

I can still remember my fellow scouts who could not conceal their fear of the dark but after surviving that night, everyone was talking about how brave we were facing the imagined ghosts and apparitions. The truth is, many of the boy scouts may have quit that night if not for peer pressure and the sense of security knowing that there were a number of us in that forlorn place.

Like an ember, this early experience grew into a flame of optimism enabling me to act unhesitatingly in the face of uncertainties. Later, even the rains or storms did not intimidate me, nor did I allow them to deter me from my plans on any given day.

*

My first experience of being alone in the dark happened when my father left me on the hard leather seat of a bicycle. It was parked in a dirt yard next to the open window of a house which

---

[22] Sexual attraction to children who have not yet reached puberty.

was not much bigger than a hut. The light from the petromax[23] illuminated me to the full view of two men inside the house. One of them was my father who was reading a book and explaining it to the other man who talked, using his finger to emphasise his point. My shadow fell on the ground on the rear of the bicycle and beyond the shadow, all was darkness. Only the sounds of their voices, dogs barking, and crickets penetrated the night.

I came to learn later that these nights were review sessions on the Bible about their incipient sect, the *Iglesia ni Cristo*,[24] when my father and his colleague, Ka [25]Pedro, were preparing for Sunday worships. Ka Pedro was the son of a Justice of the Peace who was one of the first members of their fledgling church. His grandson Adriel, who became a student activist, was reunited with me much later as a detainee during the martial law. Adriel wrote the only history of the province of La Union, which, incidentally, was my father's first big assignment as a minister in the church.

From that nipa hut, Ka Pedro later became the first missionary of the *Iglesia ni Cristo* in Hawaii, United States and from there the members grew worldwide around the world. Another minister in their early circle, Ka Lino, later followed Ka Pedro, but before that, he was seconded to my father in the province of Zambales as a training ground for his eventual overseas assignment.

It was not the combined darkness and the eerie silence that

---

[23] Brand name for a type of pressurised paraffin lamp.

[24] Independent non-trinitarian Christian church, founded and registered by Felix Y. Manalo in 1914.

[25] Tagalog word for sibling which is used for both men and women. This is how *Iglesia ni Cristo* members call one another as an append to the name.

was broken intermittently by the sound of barking dogs and chirping crickets or the voices coming from the house that annoyed me but the swarming mosquitoes and flying bugs. Battling with them made me forget I was alone.

I was between three and four years old at that time.

This was the late 1940s in Urdaneta, Pangasinan, the town where my father spent most of his youth and where I spent my first four years.

I did not forget this incident because it was also the first time that I felt guilty. On the way home, my father made me sit on the bicycle's iron bar between him and the handlebars. He let me hold the Bible and I held it tightly while he was pumping the pedals. On those rides back home, he would tell me biblical stories, one of which was about a box which the Jews were instructed by God not to touch because it was holy and anyone who touched it would surely die regardless of whether their motive for touching the box was good or bad.

God's caution must be observed, no more, no less, he emphasised as if I already knew the weight or value of things. God's words must be spread, he said, and this is why we frequently visited houses at night. He was always welcome in these homes which mostly belonged to the members of his church and while interacting with them, he let me sit on his bicycle outside the house but in his view most of the time.

The long wait for him to finish his missionary work every evening taught me patience. For the first time also, I looked at the sky and learnt addition by counting the stars above and thought that someday I may reach one of them. But my father told me that somewhere there lies heaven or paradise for those who obey God's words. His description of paradise excited my newly acquired consciousness.

I thought then that the Bible, which he said contained the words of God, must be held with utmost care. Of course, it should be held with care but there is another context of what I said. It was my first lesson on God's word and the sanctity of the Bible as well. On one ride home, I was holding the Bible clumsily and in a short while, it fell from my hands. My father did not reprimand me but simply picked it up and gave it back to me. But remembering the story about the box and God's instruction to take care of it gave me nightmares for many nights. I was consumed with worry that God might punish me for dropping His book. Later, my father told me that he was referring not to the Bible but to the Ark of the Covenant, [26] which the Jews carried in their travels from place to place.

I was relieved to know that I was not cursed after all. I learnt how it is to feel guilty from the experience of dropping the Bible.

If we were not riding together on the bicycle, we would walk at night with my elder brother holding a petromax to light our path. These were long walks to places where he would join a crowd of ten to twenty people where there would be singing and reading of the Bible. On our way home, our father would point at places where he had some relatives or friends or where a dog would pursue him. He said that at first, he was scared but later he would just ignore the dog and it would stop barking and stop pursuing him.

"Do not show the dog that you are scared," he said. I did not realise then that he was initiating me to the psychology of dogs which also reflects the conduct of some human beings.

---

[26] Gold-covered wooden chest containing the tablet of stone where the Ten Commandments were inscribed.

He showed me and my brother how to whistle by placing two fingers inside the mouth to produce a sound, a trick I was never able to master. He said it could be a signal that one is in distress or in danger and would invite a rescue or protection.

I thought then that our father was just distracting us from the darkness with such a banal and folksy exercise but later I learnt that whistling was a stand-alone language among the folks in such distant land as in Kuskoy, Turkey[27] where the folks use this medium to communicate over long distances. Even today, the UNESCO is exerting efforts to preserve such a unique form of communication.

I could whistle but the sound was so feeble that it required complete silence to hear it. I was dismayed at myself, while my elder brother could whistle high and long. Later, my brother and I split these nightly lessons; my brother fancied whistling and I was interested in reading the Bible. We did not know then that this nocturnal training would lead us into separate interests in life.

For example, when we were in our teens, my brother would hear deep in the night a whistled sound and he would whistle back and then I would see him tiptoeing out of our house to meet his 'barkada'. [28] Whistling served as their communication, their version of a Morse code to avoid detection from vigilant parents. My brother enjoyed the adventure with his friends and the experience of joy from the camaraderie made him a social person for the rest of his life.

---

[27] Village in Turkey where whistling has been the mode of long-distance communication for 400 years.

[28] Tagalog word for a close friend or group of friends.

\*

The sorties at night whether just walking with my father or riding with him on his bicycle paid off. Five or seven years later when we lived in Santiago, Isabela[29] for his ministerial assignment, my father would ask me at night to buy his cigarette at Centro, so-called because it is the centre of town. Actually, then an imported cigarette was a luxury and so depending on the state of his finances there were times he would instruct me to buy dried and refined Virginia tobacco leaves and cigarette foils instead which I helped roll to make a cigarette.

Centro was more than a kilometre away from our house passing through a road that was already deserted by people who have retired for the night, and savannah with thick foliage at the back of an elementary school and where *'narra'*[30] and *'banaba'*[31] trees made a little forest. Sometimes, the errand at night is for his favourite *'Sy Hok Tong'*[32] or *Syoktong*, a Chinese alcohol with herbal roots. It was not long before I was attracted by the aroma coming from the bark or roots mixed with the alcohol and at first, I had a little sip out of curiosity. Later I was sharing it with my father, but I was careful to just sip a negligible amount to prolong the supply and avoid detection.

I don't think my father had suspected our shared interest although he noticed in me a better appetite at every meal since

---

[29] Now a city about 326 kilometers north of Manila.

[30] National tree of the Philippines.

[31] Tree in the Philippines, the leaves of which are commonly used as herbal medicine.

[32] Chinese herbal wine.

that time. The clean air and walk at night are a good exercise and when the blood flows freely the appetite is enhanced and it makes a person lively, he commented. I suspected that deep inside he had really intended to make me a brave man and adlibbing about health as his rationale in these nocturnal missions was just a convenient screen.

He also instructed me to wrap the bottle with an old newspaper page as soon as I receive the *Syoktong* bottle from the sales help of the Chinese store. It was a precaution because of a strict church policy against drinking alcohol of any measure. I did my errand in a surreptitious and mysterious way to shield my father from any negative talk about him—a provincial chief executive minister of his church taking a drink with alcohol content would erode his credibility and authority. For a good length of time, I suffered the suspicious thought of my father breaking church policy but later I found out that it was my mother who was mixing the bark and roots together with the diluted alcohol in the bottle of *Syoktong*. It was not at all an alcoholic spirit. She too was into it and not much later she was pregnant with our youngest sibling who turned out to be the only girl. Eavesdropping one day, I heard my mother prescribing a friend who had been childless for seven years a sip of *Syoktong* to hope for a child. This was my first encounter with the so-called herbal medicine. The drink served my father well, making him active and buoyant with a lot of positive attitudes.

*

That savannah going to and from Centro also had a single tamarind tree at the centre. The tree's spot actually

56

commanded a big space where every summer the youth held sports activities like volleyball, softball, basketball and track— and-field competitions. The youth looked forward to these summer tilts where sportsmanship and camaraderie were encouraged.

But I had a different kind of sport during times when the place was deserted, and the land was dry. Usually, I would saunter around that vacant place at two o'clock in the afternoon with my dog which I named *Fighter*. Fighter would run around and egg me on to throw a stick for him so he could run after it and bring it back to me. Fighter actually is a reincarnation of English, another dog I had in San Fernando, La Union which was the previous place my father had been assigned. English saved my life when I was sleepwalking, and in that state, I was about to cross the national highway when English pulled to stop me by biting at my pants with his strong teeth. When we were in Santiago, Isabela my father looked for a dog that resembled English but to set him apart I called him Fighter. It seemed that Fighter lived through his name unlike English who died of loneliness after we left him in San Fernando, La Union.[33]

Fighter's concentration was distracted when there are other people passing by and he would scare them away as if he wanted me to own the place for myself. He would look furious showing his fangs when it was only an old man passing by holding an empty sack. He may have heard my mother telling me about some boys who went missing and never came back because they were taken by some foul elements. It was a time

---

[33] At that time a 3rd class municipality along the shore of La Union facing the China Sea.

when the recruitment of teens was in full swing for the underground insurgents fighting the government.

It was hard to keep pace with Fighter so I would lie down to rest. Looking up I would see and admire the clouds and the vastness of space, asking myself what lies behind those clouds and blue space, while my dog was just resting his head on his paws watching me or pursuing a female canine that had attracted his attention. Fighter's attraction to the opposite sex had opened my eyes to my own attraction to the female species.

It was while being half-awake and half-asleep enjoying a peaceful bliss in that savannah when a teen showed up from the direction of Centro taking that route as a shortcut to where he was going. I was caught by surprise when he stopped where I was daydreaming with my back on the ground looking at the sky. When he settled, Fighter was uncharacteristically silent like he was cowed or even disinterested.

My reaction was contemporaneous to my experience the night before at the forested area nearby. On my way back from the Chinese store there was a light and smoke from the treetop and a scary sound. There had always been stories about black spirits called 'kapre'[34] that caused the weak-hearted among us kids to avoid the area. As a safeguard, I would always bring my slingshot and when I felt a presence, I loaded it and shot at the flickering light emanating from the leaves in one of the higher branches. I was about to bolt from the place when I heard the sound of a human cry. The 'kapre' turned out to be my brother and his friends.

---

[34] In Philippine folklore, he is a tobacco-puffing giant that lives on old giant trees.

\*

"You have a nice dog," the intruder said to strike up conversation. This young man was no *kapre* but my experience the night before left a lingering feeling that the area was inhabited by spirits from another dimension who could materialise at any given moment. As a young boy's psyche is shaped by folk stories endemic in one's culture, I regarded this newcomer in that context.

This was the first time I'd met someone with a fair complexion and his eyes were slit giving his expression one of intensity. He regarded me with a certain familiarity until I realised that he was the boy of my age, a Chinese-Filipino at the grocery where I bought my father's drink tonic. He was an enigma to me at first but looking at the trees and the sky and the whole universe of nature around us with the same eye and appreciation at that moment, revealed a human being who was both warm and dreamy. That early, I realised how similar we were although there were differences in the colour of our skin and culture.

He threw a stone at a bunch of low-hanging ripe tamarind fruits. Bullseye! The next thing I knew my new friend and I shared a feast of sweet tamarind fruit. Fighter showed his approval as he approached my new friend licking at his shoes with his tail wagging but refusing the tamarind seeds thrown his way. Chen is no ne'er-do-well.[35]

This encounter with the stranger became a learning experience and a big influence in my life. He pointed out a

---

[35] Not lazy nor irresponsible.

stone house at the other end of the big clearing which was shrouded by a thick canopy of overgrown and unpruned butterfly bush aligned with the wire fence with its beautiful cone-shaped flowers.

I had always passed by that house on one of my night-time errands, taking the opposite side of the road because I thought it was abandoned and a haunted house. Instead, he convinced me that he had business in the place, and he said that it would be good and productive for me if I joined him. To disabuse my mind, he pointed out that the owner of the house likes his privacy and enjoys the peace afforded by the hedge of shrubs that made the house looked isolated. The house had always been an object of my curiosity and I'd long wanted to peep inside.

The decision to leave my comfort zone around the tamarind tree was one of many in my early teens like the events that I will share with you subsequently...

\*

A week before I met Chen in my savannah while daydreaming, I was invited on a joyride in an auto calesa or passenger jeepney that was plying the Santiago-Ilagan [36] route. Just imagine the fire of reckless abandon among three teens, the driver, conductor and myself with one or two years between each other, but I was the youngest. We picked up passengers along the way but because of the long distance, we did not have passengers most of the way. The driver would really drive the vehicle in a fit of daredevil madness in the stretch passing

[36] A 94-km road in Isabela province.

by expansive rice fields of Cagayan Valley. [37] It was exhilarating and our inexperience made us oblivious of the dangers that could possibly happen if the driver made an emergency stop, the brake mechanism of the vintage MacArthur-type jeep[38] broke, or we lost our grip and fell. The round trip between Santiago and Ilagan over a very rough gravel road would take us almost a day as we negotiated the route in a part-leisure and part-work fashion. The high point of the trip was when our vehicle was chartered by a farmer somewhere in the town of Cauayan[39] to bring his corn to the market of Ilagan. He had been waiting for hours for transport to load his produce. He promised to pay us for the freight as soon as he dispatched his produce to the retailers. We helped in the loading and unloading of the corn in sacks and waited for him to finish his transaction. On the way back, he invited us to stop by his farm where we met his family. We spent a little time with him bantering like we were old friends and I asked him why not just wait for middlemen to pick up his produce. He told me that he gets more value for his crops if he sells direct in the market. He knew his economics and just lacked the opportunity to capitalise. On our way home he loaded a sack of corn in our vehicle visibly pleased with our service and company.

We were fortunate that no accident happened, but the adventure left me very appreciative of my province's richness and the land made productive by the industry of the Ilocano migrants which made Cagayan Valley the rice granary of the

---

[37] An administrative region in northern Philippines.

[38] Military surplus jeep used during the war and re-cycled by Filipinos as convenient vehicle.

[39] A 3rd —class municipality then, now a city.

Philippines. Such an impression inspired the vision and creativity that enriched my contributions to agricultural reforms of the countryside many years later. It was particularly pleasant and lasting to my friend, the driver, in a personal way. He visited the farmer again and again until he got married to the farmer's eldest daughter who became a teacher as well as my friend.

*

I think nothing would compare in adventure and drama with another experience I had when I visited the place of my birth in San Manuel, Pangasinan when I was ten years old.

It was summer vacation and I remember my mother taking me to the bus station that would take me directly from Santiago, Isabela to Binalonan in Pangasinan, ten hours away of land travel a town along the national highway on the way to Baguio City, the summer capital of the Philippines which is just an hour away up to the mountain on a zigzagging road.

Binalonan is the whistle-stop for those who would go eastward to San Manuel and other towns like the neighbouring Asingan town, the birthplace of a future president, Fidel Valdez Ramos.[40] It was the year 1956 and nine years later, Ramos' cousin, Ferdinand Marcos[41] of Ilocos Norte[42] would be elected the president of the country. Also, Binalonan is the hometown of the Macaraeg family whose daughter had become a Doctor of Medicine and later married Diosdado

---

[40] 12th President of the Philippines (1992-1998) commonly called FVR.
[41] 10th President of the Philippines (1965-1986).
[42] A province in northern Luzon.

Macapagal who also became a president of the Philippines before Marcos did. From that marriage, came a daughter, Gloria, who would become a vice president and later president of The Philippines. I would serve Gloria as the Chief of the Office of the Government Corporate Counsel in her presidency. It is refreshing that in that dot of a place in the Philippine map, national leaders would grow like seeds thrown in fertile soil.

My visit to San Manuel was most welcome to my cousins but no one would be happier than my mother's elder sister, a spinster who doted on me and another cousin, the eldest son of their youngest sister. These were happy vacation days and were mostly about swimming at the back of my aunt's house where there was clean, mostly shallow rushing water in a narrow river in the back yard that separated it from the vast farmlands on the other side. The rapids would be a summer delight as we could float on a banana trunk that would carry us downstream a good distance away from the house and just as the river would turn into a tiny stony shallow we would disembark in the back yard of another cousin's house.

Then my real experience began: the rite of passage to manhood I would experience on this visit. Our distant cousin, Manong[43] Flor, had shaped a sturdy guava twig into a stick like an anvil as his operating platform in the ritual of circumcision rite beside the clean, running river. Before the operation, he made the young boys chew guava leaves and spit on the fresh cut on the foreskin as an antibiotic. To ensure against infection, we boiled the guava leaves daily to wash the wound until it healed. Although Manong Flor was known in town to operate

---

[43] Tagalog word used to refer to a person older in age as a sign of respect.

as a psychic surgeon, he preferred to do the cutting with a sharp razor. He believed that faith is not involved when it comes to the matter of cutting the skin of man's reproductive tool. After all, it was not a religious thing like the Jewish or Islamic rite.

Compare the Filipino way to the Jewish circumcision rite in Rome, 16 January 1645 in the eyewitness account of John Evelyn:

*"The Infant now strip'd from the belly downewards, the Jew tooke the yard of the child and Chaf'd it within his fingers till it became a little stiff, then with the silver Instrument before describ'd (which was held to him in the basin) he tooke up as much of the Praeputium as he could possibly gather, and so with the Razor, did rather Saw, than citt it off; at which the miserable baby cry'd extremely, whiles the rest continu'd their odd tone, rather like howling than singing: then the Rabby lifting the belly of the child to his face, and taking the yard all blody into his mouth he suck'd it a pretty while, having before taken a little Vinegar, all which together with the blood he spitout into a glasse of red wine of the Colour of French wine. This don stripped downe the remainder of the fore-skin as farr and neere to the belly as he could, so as it appeared to be all raw, then he strew'd the read powder on it to stanch the bleeding and coverd it with the paperhood, and upon all a Clowre, and so swath'd up the Child as before: All this while they continue their Psalme: Then two of the Women, and two men, viz., he who held the child, and the Rabbin who Circumcis'd it (the rest I suppose were the Witnesses) dranke some of the Wine mingl'd with the Vinegar, blood and spittle: so ended the slovenly ceremony, and the Rabbin cryes out to me in the Italian tongue perceiving me to be a stranger: 'Eco*

*Signior mio, Un Miracolo di dio'; because the child had immediately left crying: xxx"[44]*

This narrative of the Jewish circumcision rite explained to me why there are expletives against the Jewish detractors about their being "??? suckers".

No one suffered from his operations. When the healing is complete the boys would go swim in the same river where barrio lasses are washing their laundry, walk ramrod straight with a gait boasting that down there is the key to populate the world. There is a feast of drinking fresh coconut water to go with freshwater fish and shells taken along the bamboo-lined banks.

In the decades that would pass, the enchantment of the river would be lost when the source would be emptied into a big dam, now called San Roque Dam, [45] which would be the source of hydroelectric power that contributes substantially to the national power grid.

That river was not the only casualty of the need for electricity but also the mountain nearby which hosts another of my fondest memories.

During that same vacation, our aunt brought me and my younger cousin on a mountain trek which begun with us taking a horse-drawn calesa to as far as it was possible to navigate. The mountain trek was another two hours under the morning sun.

Our aunt was extremely excited to bring us there to check on her investment and along the way she was telling us that

---

[44] From the book EYEWITNESS TO HISTORY Edited by John Carey, p. 179.

[45] Largest dam in the Philippines and now 16th largest in the world.

she had bought a heifer[46] several months before and was speculating that the female calf would be ready for a mate now. She started to do the math. She said that soon she would give us a calf each. She imagined that if they are raised on the ranch, we could expect to be owners of a dozen of those calves. My cousin and I started to share our dreams with each other, and I told him that I'd want a horse so I could ride over the mountain after my calves just like a cowboy.

When we started going downhill, our aunt pointed to a small clearing where some people were congregating as though they were celebrating a special event. From the way she spoke, her excitement was contagious with high expectations of good news about her investment. Upon reaching the clearing, she asked for the farm leader to whom she had entrusted her calf. When the farm leader met us, he showed no welcome cheer but told my aunt about how her calf had died the month before. I saw the great disappointment on the tired and perspiring face of our aunt, as if all her hopes vanished with the bad news. After offering us lunch with a butchered young calf which my aunt suspected to be *her* calf, we went back the same way and the trek seemed to be longer with the sun withdrawing its light from us to make me sadder for my aunt.

I did not know then that the place was a secret rustler's lair and I had come face to face with desperate men who may have spared our lives to atone for my aunt's loss after what would have been our last lunch. Later, I reflected on the calf giving its life for us and why, perhaps, some religion or cult had venerated a calf or other animal because of a life-saving

---

[46] A young female cow that has not borne a calf.

experience.

*

My new friend Chen, the huckster, and I made a call on the house together. In this ensuing speck of time, I learnt much about human behaviour, the laws of nature and an experience that was universally relevant. Later, at law school, I found a ready example of the legal principles being discussed by our professors because of the déjà vu feelings from this afternoon in my boyhood.

After we entered the open gate, I saw a lush tropical green on both sides of the big front lawn. There were hardy banana trees on the right perimeter going into the front door. On the left perimeter was a single guava tree and two guyabano[47] trees with fruits that were raw, green, elongated and pointed rough skin, hanging low towards the ground, a picture of nature which made me relate easily to the phrase "low-hanging fruits" many years later. I thought it was a wilderness until my scent led my gaze to a bed of roses on the catwalk whose bouquet of flowers made a good impression of the hand that daily tends to them.

My new friend didn't seem to notice this display of nature, but it turned out to be a feigned disinterest when I heard him comment about the homeowner's fastidiousness but nevertheless kind-hearted and nature-loving manner. At that point, I did not have any inkling of our business and just went with the flow. Every step we took towards the front door was carried with confidence which was helped by my innocence

---

[47] Soursop

about our business and my attention to the foliage around.

When I had enough interaction with the world outside, I realised that my friend and business partner was priming himself so that by his actions and even facial expression he could project a positive attitude that would influence a favourable response from the owner of the house. My friend's demeanour was partly enlightened by what a poker player or even any player in contact games do to make the other players react or lower their guard favourably to the intended play sought by the adroit playmaker. The turn of events which unfolded afterwards in the course of our objective in visiting the house showed that my friend's positive attitude was reciprocated.

I saw again in close quarters in the ensuing years how this kind of attitude brings tremendous success to one who employs this ruse like a professional foul in soccer to deprive another of an advantage. When I confronted one who would feign his actions, he says that it takes skill to do it in face-to-face encounters or when confronted with an event where there is a multiplicity of people acting to pursue cross purposes.

At law school many years after the fact, I asked our professor in legal ethics whether or not this feigning or concealing one's thoughts in any transaction would be considered unethical per se. He asked me to be more specific as ethics is not an exact science and the answer would vary depending on the circumstances. He gave the class a roundabout answer. He explained that an overt act being external means that it therefore can be weighed and judged while pure intention which exists merely in the mind is a prerogative and its range is unlimited even to the extent of being lascivious, criminal or irreverent.

Our professor expanded on the subject when he added that the role of the mind of an angry or aggrieved victim raring to get even is like an exhaust built in to make the energy of his negative emotions released internally hurting no one. He cited the Japanese practice of setting up hard walls to break glasses or ceramics against to serve as a release of pent-up rage.[48] In the absence of this mechanism, the personality is inhibited and results in psychopathy.

Without an operative act, he said, a mere intention is not to be judged as ethical or unethical. But when a bad act is done, the presence of premeditation confers to the unethical action its severity or gravity and also the duty to compensate for the consequential damage. He cautioned us against equating the legal intention in law from a sin committed merely by a thought, like a case cited by Jesus of one desiring a woman married to another. When an unacted intention becomes wrong to be punished in this world, human activity and creativity will grind to a halt.

The students reacted differently, some were confused but the others saw practical wisdom because the mere intention is hard or impossible to know and therefore it is a matter of conscience. Our professor was not only a lawyer but a psychologist, a student of human tendencies rolled into one. When businessmen were asked, however, whose capital or business is on the line on the outcome of the transaction, they are unanimous in claiming that feigning during negotiations is an acceptable tool. They cited John D. Rockefeller's "quiet and dull appearance" when making a grab of someone's

---

[48] Called Rage Room, although it is usually an open area which is adopted by many countries.

business that enabled him to monopolise the oil refinery in the United States.

It kept the students thinking about ethics from many points of view, one from the point of view of the law, another from the practical sense among businessmen, and thirdly, from the pure ethics of the great teacher, Jesus. We were confused to learn that there is no universal ethical standard to guide us. Then our law professor said that we should not think that ethics is relative according to one's suit. You have to understand a person and the way he pursues his interest. He may engage one with humility or he may engage another with pride. But both humility and pride could be extremes and it would be better to follow the middle way. So, in the case of humility and pride, it is better to be modest. Between secrecy and loquacity is honesty; between being the quarrelsome one and the flatterer, showing friendship is the ethical way. Aristotle[49] called this the Golden Mean. Our professor advised us to learn from the motto inscribed on the temple of Apollo at Delphi: *"Meden Agan"* or "nothing in excess"! He cited the Greek proverb, "It is dangerous to eat too little but also to eat too much," he summed up the ethical standard as the balance of things.

*

I felt my new friend and I were welcome at the house because after only a slight tap on the door it was opened by a man whom I assumed to be the master of the house. The instant cordiality and somewhat warm welcome impressed me of the good nature of the host and that put us at ease.

---

[49] The Greek Philosopher.

It was a fine Saturday afternoon and the man, who was about the age of my father, was in a comfortable casual shirt paired with striped pyjama pants and leather slippers. His mood was friendly, and I assumed he had just taken his siesta which had temporarily unburdened him of worldly woes. He was holding a book and he smiled at me approvingly when he saw me looking intently at the title. I saw his delight in me the way my father let me hold his Bible. This book is a story of philosophy, and he mentioned the author which I forgot for a long time but not the title of the book.

My writer-friend at the canteen in Manila had advised me many years later to read Will Durant's *Story of Philosophy*[50] which prompted me to recall this episode.

Anyway, the kind man told me that reading classics like Tolstoy[51] would widen one's perspective and the way you think about many things like God, the universe, and the nature of men. John Locke[52] and Thomas Hobbes[53] inform you on humanities, he added, pointing at the titles of the open books on the small table by a sofa. The big wall on one side of the living room was lined with many books on literature which, according to him, would stir your feelings while reading and fighting vicariously difficult battles that imitate life. I saw Fyodor Dostoyevsky's[54] *The Brother Karamazov* already in

---

[50] American historian and philosopher who won a Pulitzer Prize for his *Story of Civilization*.

[51] Russian writer regarded as one of the greatest authors of all time.

[52] English philosopher and physician and "Father of Liberalism".

[53] English philosopher considered to be one of the founders of modern political philosophy.

[54] Russian novelist and short-story writer; author of *Crime and Punishment* and *The Brothers Karamazov*.

tatters. Predominantly, there were shelves of uniformly covered books titled 'PHILIPPINE REPORTS', a compilation of the decisions of the Philippine Supreme Court printed in the books' spines.

On top of the line of books was a name-plate which identified the owner as a lawyer and notary public. There were no images of saints in the house nor any article of veneration as was prevalent in many Filipino households. It seemed that our host's fancy for books had spared him from worshiping idols.

Then our host turned his attention to my friend who was busy taking from his little bag a shoe polish container and a small piece of clean white cloth. He turned his eyes to me and my friend one after the other twice as if he were seeing two paths for each of us, one just initiated to the world of books while the other destined for the rough business world.

My partner then asked permission to rub the wooden table with his polishing cream leaving a portion untouched until the rest of the tabletop was covered with what he called a magic cleaner. I was in awe at how it had even removed rough marks caused by objects being carelessly placed on top. The table now shined as if it were a brand-new table. This side was in sharp contrast to the portion of the table left unpolished: proof of the effectiveness of his magic cream.

This incident cast a shadow of events to fast forward. When I was at law school, our law professor in the subject of Evidence asked for a clear example of *'res ipsa loquitur'*.[55] I cited that polished tabletop as proof of the effectivity of the polishing cream, but he was unimpressed and told the class

---

[55] Latin for "The thing speaks for itself".

that in a casual sense it fits the concept but not in a forensic sense which sounded too technical for me.

Anyway, my friend did more than relying heavily upon the polished table. To further impress, he started to clean a one-foot statuette lording over the centre of the table only to be restrained by the man of the house who told him not to apply anything on it because it will ruin its value as an antique piece. In this category of things, he said, the rust is part of their value. When the old glitter goes, it will no longer be gold, the lawyer added, which reminded me of my father's similar advice.

My friend concluded the sales presentation and after quoting the price of a big tin container of the polishing wax he said that he was leaving a sample and would make a return visit the following day for the host's decision. The kind man did not reject the offer, but his response was far from reassuring. I assumed that he thought the price was outrageous which I shared but kept my opinion to myself and hoped for the best.

I knew we failed but even before we could leave, we heard the house-help cry from the back of the house with excitement. The host rushed to the back yard holding our departure in abeyance and when he came back, he was cradling a big grey cat. The man of the house explained that they had left the cat on their farm in another town a week ago and the cat had been missing ever since. But apparently the cat had traced the road back to the house and it was to his great relief that it was unscathed except that it was littered with dust. It was not grey after all but a beautiful white cat.

Our host educated us, in such good spirits and breathlessly in a long-winded talk about cats being good pets, giving significance to the fact that cats have a homing trait which is the ability to trace their steps back to their home even if lost at a great distance and this trait eventually ballyhooed their many lives. He added with a toothy smile: "Avoid bringing home a kitten if you are not serious."

The rejoicing brought by the prodigal cat was a cause for my friend and myself to be particularly ecstatic. When the host calmed after being euphoric, he asked for a discount on the price of the polished wax. My friend winked at me in triumph. Looking at me, he took a long pause which may have been misunderstood as a hesitation at meeting the discounted offer. That momentary pause was interrupted by the host offering to buy instead two tin containers at the discounted price. I have seen later many procrastinations that ended in disaster but this one turned out to be a success. I loved cats. They always reminded me of that white polish and the dust-covered cat who snatched us from the jaws of failure and delivered the biggest financial success of my childhood.

Then he turned to me. "Say hello to your father. I have not seen him for a while."

I looked at my friend and he was smiling from ear to ear with the revelation that I'd been his ticket to enter the house.

"Boys, keep up a good heart. It will bring you good fortune and happiness to those you touch!"

Later, my reconciliation with my father would not be unlike the owner's happiness at the return of his prodigal cat.

I wondered where his words of spirituality came from when there is not even any evidence of religiosity in and outside his home! They may have flowed from the cool green hedge around the house which offers protection from the harsh heat of the summer sun.

These were his serendipitous send-off words. He may

have considered our visit as a good omen. Though he was a few pesos poorer as a consequence of our sales coup, the charity in his heart with his advice made him grand in our eyes.

I returned to my present situation when the beautiful nurse pushed the curtain around my bed open and as she touched my forehead, the recollection of my childhood and teen years closed with her warmth. She was smiling sweetly in return to what she mistook as an admiring thought, but the truth is I was just enjoying my memories of the funny notion about the dog, the calf, and the polished cat, whose role in my life I have recalled earlier, could qualify them as the centre of veneration in a nescient, itsy-bitsy cult.

I went to sleep peacefully and soundly in my hospital bed, the first rest I'd had since arriving in Manila. In my hand, tightly gripped was the envelope from Manny as though it were my first twenty pesos, my share that eidetic day in Santiago, Isabela.

# 3
# A FOOL'S ERRAND

Two months earlier!

The unprecedented success of my joint venture with the huckster was a tour de force, propelling me towards my choice to leave home. I have to admit, though, that the dice were loaded against me. I was frail, sickly and underweight. I was too young and wet behind the ears to have pulled that kind of stunt. What the heck? That deficiency did not deter me from 'ruling the roost'.[56]

*

When I reached the provincial bus station in Santiago, my ride to Manila was already warming its diesel engine. I was relieved that there was no obstacle to my escape so far but still I did not choose one of the front seats to avoid being discovered at once. Besides, the back seat at the end of the bus compartment was more appealing as a bed for sleep during the estimated twelve-hour trip.

My guilt over running away from home was made worse by a previous incident in third-year high school which almost ended in a disaster for our rover scout troop in an out-of-town

---

[56] An idiom meaning someone who prevails.

sally.

Our troop took a bus ride from the town of Santiago to the town of San Agustin to the east of the Province of Isabela. When we started the bus trip very early in the morning, the sun rose to promise good weather for the entire trip. But upon reaching the town of Jones next to San Agustin, we were surprised to find the weather so bad with incessant rain and the downpour so thick and long there was almost zero visibility. Our scoutmaster started to fidget.

We soon found out why.

The river at the boundary of Jones and San Agustin had overflowed because it had been raining intermittently the night before. The bridge over the river and the only way to our destination was no ordinary bridge but not a modern structure either. The planks that formed the road were laid over big logs and could only accommodate one-way traffic. In addition, guard railings were missing from either side.

The scoutmaster wisely decided to rest the bus at the approach of the bridge, and we all went down when the rain subsided and the water over the bridge emptied. We scouted the area out and concluded that the wooden bridge was in no danger of being swept away. The problem was the river was still raging from floodwaters coming from the nearby mountain and the current was not only swift but had a whirlpool. As a precaution, we decided to walk over the bridge, a distance of about one hundred metres to lighten the busload.

As we walked single file, the scout ahead of me tripped. I extended my hand which he held but our combined weight and his desperate pull caused us to teeter on the edge. We were fortunate that a bigger scout was able to grab my khaki pants which did not give way. The scout on the outer edge was able to gain his footing to safety on the bridge's floor.

Looking back to that experience, it told me how symbolic that scene was with me extending my hand for my half-Chinese friend, the one with me under the tamarind tree, and the bigger half-Indian classmate extending his hand to me as well, a cooperation that saved us from an almost fatal outcome.

The excursion ended well with everyone in the troop feeling triumphant over the challenge from the weather and the forbidding terrain. The rainbow that showed over the mountain brightened our prospects for the day and optimism prevailed over our justified fears. There were exaggerated talks of triumph afterwards among the boys and the bigger the feat, the greater was the boost to our confidence. It was scouting psychology at its best.

I was euphoric and my sharing of the incident with my mother was animated. Her instant reaction of relief was more a motherly instinct. Later, she thought of many 'ifs' had the incident turned worse. Then she would express regret having allowed me to join the excursion without having consulted with my father. Since then, consulting with my father and the spectre of a bad omen was a cause and effect which my mother embraced like the feeling provoked by a black cat crossing the pathway. [57] In leaving home without my father's consent or even making an escape would be much worse!

*

There were people moving around the bus station waiting for

---

[57] A superstitious belief considered to be a bad omen!

their rides while others passed by on the way to the market or to the farm or home from a night shift. It was a routine for them in this small town. These people may enjoy peace of mind, all right, but I will be equally blessed with the youthful thrill of living alone in the city far from home I thought. But it was not pleasure that I was seeking but experience and the delight of the mind.

Sitting there in the ill-ventilated bus inhaling a dose of diesel smoke, I was fighting my sagging morale with a declamation[58] piece I recited in an interclass contest in second-year high school. The epic line eludes me. It must be because of guilt, or fear of the unknown, or excitement of freedom but it took two or three attempts before I remembered and succeeded in putting the captain and the master in the right combination with 'my soul' and 'my fate'.

"I am the master of my fate, I am the captain of my soul".[59]

Our venerated English teacher did not warn us that we would be fools to swallow the phrase hook, line, and sinker. She was wise to leave the discovery of the pitfalls of such bold and dreamy ideas to us in a hard and enriching way. Whatever her shortcomings in this regard, she and Willian Ernest Henley, living centuries apart, have successfully conspired to create that chutzpah in the youth which Ernest Renan, [60] a French philosopher, and biblical scholar had described as natural of that age being "borne with imprecations on the lips".

It was five o'clock in the morning when the bus finally

---

[58] Artistic form of public speaking competition in school; Dramatic oration.
[59] Invictus by poet William Ernest Henley.
[60] A French historian of religion (1823-1892).

left the Santiago, Isabela bus terminal.

The bus ride on the bumpy highway is a trope of a different kind of a journey fuelled in part by a drive to go ahead in life and in equal weight by that oversized curiosity of a boy to discover the vast world like a domesticated cub set free from a fenced den into the wild.

My pulse quickened when I saw the bus conductor approaching the back seat with a heavyset bald man in tow. I recognised the man. I liked Tata Abon, the janitor of our chapel in front of the ministerial house.

For a moment there was a feeling of welcome relief in case he was there to tell me that my father sent him to get me back. The comfort of home is still tempting and the urge to return is encouraged by the fear of the unknown. My father had never failed me, and I can leave my future entirely in his hands. Besides, there is a comfortable simplicity in his household like the security and predictability of starting every morning with a pleasant brew like chamomile tea to calm the mind. But if this trip will not push through, then there are no more dreams and no hopes as well. In that split second, I became resolved by my realisation that I had reached the point of no return.

Tata Abon's presence is a reassuring send-off. I had spent many hours keeping him company while he was cleaning the chapel. He made a good janitor, polishing all the wooden floors especially the 'tribuna' or pulpit where the ministers deliver their Thursdays and Sunday's sermons.

When I was not home and not in school, I was always with Tata Abon. Sometimes his wife, Nana Ingga, also helped him clean the chapel. I was not particularly fond of Nana Ingga because there is something sinister in the way she looks.

Whenever I thought of a witch, her image comes to mind. Her eyes are piercing, so penetrating that I would perspire in fear. There was something in her right eye that tends to widen her vision right wise that even if she appears looking at me straight ahead with her left eye, she is also admiringly watching Tata Abon with her other eye. She would only remove her gaze after she spat out the betel nut she was always chewing.

Later my friends told me in jest that only a watchful and extremely jealous woman could perform such a trick with her eyes. Even my wife resented being compared to Nana Ingga. She does not resemble Nana Ingga physically, but her way of rejecting any insinuation of being jealous or too protective calls the woman to mind.

But there is certain pleasantness that permeates the air with affection whenever they are together. They seem not to be bothered by the circumstance of their low life as long as they were with each other. It is love enhanced by the tonic of the floor wax, the dirt on the ground notwithstanding. Later, I would discover that their love came from something deeper. I thought they were childless.

My initial disaffection with Nana Ingga was perhaps due to the fact that Tata Abon was a very good storyteller, and our storytelling time was always cut short when Nana Ingga appeared. She always pushed Tata Abon to finish his work so they can walk home to a marital bliss which is in another barrio[61] quite far from the chapel. But Nana Ingga had her own spell on me; her magic of cooking up native delicacies. It is a mixed feeling, a juvenile ambivalence of fear due to the intense ambiguity of her gaze, or my guilt that she could feel

---

[61] Sub-unit of a local government outside of the municipal centre.

my resentment when she intrudes in our storytelling moments, but then subdued by the delights from mouth-watering home-cooked desserts. She bought my endearment of her, at first it was transactional, but then it became a genuine feeling as the company of Tata Abon became incomplete without her.

I was about ten years old when I first met Tata Abon. He warned me not to leave footprints on the 'tribuna' where he always cleaned with a homemade wax that left it shiny. He would scare me whenever he told me about some strange noise he heard while cleaning at four o'clock in the morning. He can heal with his hand and can fix dislocated joints. That is why he was called an *'albularyo'*. [62] He augments his meagre income from the church with his healing practice. He took it as a gift from the strangers that made the eerie sounds in the chapel. He did not want to lose that gift which accounts for the endurance, fun, and love of cleaning the church. That was how we started our friendship. It was actually a teacher-pupil relationship, with him teaching me through his strange stories which were aplenty. For a while, I fantasised about possessing the magic to heal. So, I would sometimes sit alone in the 'tribuna' hoping to hear from Tata Abon's spirits who could give me a gift like that of Tata Abon's.

Then, there was something he showed me; another reason that attracted me to visit him almost every day. It was a shell the size of a third of his palm. He told me that when he holds the shell, he holds in his hands, eternity. Then he put the shell to my ear. I could hear just a whizz which he claimed was the sound of time since the beginning of creation. He told me that we would be gone from this world, but the sound will still be

---

[62] Quack doctor.

there. I was impressed, a genuine wonder from a boy eager to learn.

He talked to me with total confidence while he brought the narra floor to a high lustre. Watching the dexterity with which he performed his task caused me to focus on what he was saying. The hypnotic spell did not cause me lasting damage because I started to be curious about things around me. He read what I was thinking and told me that he would give the oversized shell to me at the right time. The anticipation to receive the shell and his wonderful stories caused me look forward to these sessions with him.

Tata Abon was carrying a thick brown paper bag when he boarded the bus. I could see in his eyes that he was worried.

"I saw you leaving, and I followed you. I have these sweets from your Nana Ingga, banana, and some boiled eggs and sweet yams. Here is also your drinking water for the trip," he said, handing me a water container. He winked at me when he said his friends, the spirits in the 'tribuna', will join me on the trip. He knew, however, that I had outgrown his spirits, but he may be referring to the fears that will haunt me being alone in my journey. Of course, metaphors are part of his way of expressing things. When he tried to reach the boy in me, I knew he wanted to relive our days of humour together but his eyes glistened to betray the sadness of seeing me go.

With his bundle of send-off goods, I realised that I did not take my dinner and also it was breakfast time. I was relieved as well.

"When you come back, tell me some stories too."

He must have thought that this was only a temporary separation.

I was choking. I wanted to thank him, not just for the food

and water, but for his wisdom and fables. He may have been unschooled, but he was my literati of folk wisdom, like Aesop who taught through his fables.

I think he knows my unexpressed gratitude. I could feel it when he tousled my hair, with the same hand he used to fix me whenever I had a sprain or to rub my throat to remove a tiny fishbone I had inadvertently swallowed. The relief afterwards had made his presence a source of comfort and security that there was always a measure of peace whenever he was around. In that way, Tata Abon was a comforting presence in my innocence but not that morning after I had just committed my first act against the wishes of my father. In my adult life, I realised that pure peace comes from pure innocence. We cannot forever be young though, but senility would be closest to the innocence of youth.

Then Tata Abon put his hand in his pocket, and I could see him pulling out the coveted shell. But his hand stayed in his pocket and without saying anything, he abruptly turned to hide his face. I thought it was a deliberate sleight of hand to show his displeasure about my departure. But his movements were just enough for me to grasp a portrait of the emotion that caused his tears to fall. This image still lingers in that mind stream called memory. It moved me that from a man who is not even a blood relation, a rare bond connects one's youth to an old pure soul, indescribable yet the heart can understand. In later years I sought from people that kind of connection to test their genuine affinity.

I never saw him again after that brief encounter, but he left a psychological imprint second only to my parents. This bond may have been a feeling linked to my emotions or from that day which had deeply affected me; still, that feeling of being in his protective charge lingered to adulthood when one's judgement is more objective and detached.

\*

My anticipation gave way to a sound sleep despite the rumbling of the bus. When I woke up, fresh air was blowing from the open window. I feasted on the greenery; the imposing trees and vegetation in the fields and covering the mountain, made more resplendent by the morning sun. It will take me many years to see nature's art of that grandeur again. Those years when that beauty in the countryside was denied to me by work and study in Manila, my musings tell of this sight as my Isabela's, my province's, sad adieu, like a condemned man's last meal, to one who will experience the toughest battle ahead. While banking the beautiful landscape in my memory, freedom became a part of my active vocabulary.

I was just sixteen years and five months old then. What exactly did I want?

The same question had bothered my father even at an earlier age. He was ten years old when his mother died. She instilled in him the values of curiosity and understanding of people. To cope with her death, he had to be strong. He matured beyond his age. It helped that as he roamed around the town and in the fields of Urdaneta,[63] Pangasinan to seek solace from the loss of his mother, he easily identified with those who were suffering from the rampant injustice dealt by life with its existing social and economic structure that favoured the rich and powerful. Little by little, the voice within

---

[63] Back then, a town of Pangasinan, now a city.

him started to cry for justice for the people he knew and cared about.

So, at a young age, he joined a group demanding justice from landlords and usurers who took their lands as payments of debts. Even then, he saw how disadvantaged and unable the poor were to fight the high-handed ways by which the landlords and the well-connected dealt with them. His young mind was offended by the ruinous effects of the injustice making them hungry and homeless.

He sympathised and sought to correct it quoting the Bible on his side:

"Men do not despise a thief, if he steals to satisfy his soul when he is hungry. But if he is found, he shall restore sevenfold; he shall give all the substance of his house."[64]

He was always careful to connect the last sentence of the verse to correct any misunderstanding that stealing to feed the stomach is not carte blanche.[65]

It was only when he was sick and became a liability in the group's mobility that he was prevailed upon to go home. When he was already removed from the 'theatre of war', the government troops encircled their hiding place, pinned them down and with their superior arms, wiped out all those who resisted.

He believed that there was a reason why he got sick and that is because he was destined for another calling.

His older sister was bequeathed with his mother's religiosity and devotion to the Virgin Mother by going to

---

[64] Proverbs 6:30.
[65] Complete freedom to act.

church every day to pray for him when he was with the insurgents and during his illness. She helped him nourish his spiritual well-being.

It took a while before he could recover his health. When he was well, the peasant anti-government band that he had earlier joined had already disbanded and become splintered groups in the mountains. He felt a sense of loss for he found solidarity with the cause they were fighting for. His respect for the *'colorums'*[66] did not wane and he would speak with a romantic flourish of those times that they would play hide-and-seek with the government troops. In a way, I was amused with a tinge of admiration with the thought that he was a boy playing a man's game. His life as a rebel for a good cause was a cherished achievement of his youth.

*

The passenger in front of me reeked of alcohol. His snoring competed with the noise of the bus' diesel engine. He may have just visited the night houses in the Mabini district of Santiago before continuing his trip. He looked at me menacingly when the bus jolted to avoid hitting a carabao and went back to sleep.

I was not scared; in fact, I was fascinated.

I remember when I was five years old in San Fernando, La Union which was a few mountains away from Cagayan Valley and on the western coast of Luzon abutting the West Philippine Sea. The primary school where I was enrolled as a

---

[66] Messianic society which had the aim of defeating and overthrowing the colonial government of the United States in the Philippines.

first-grader was about a kilometre away from our house. Every day I had to walk the entire stretch to and from school.

In a young mind, my journey from home to school was fraught with a single danger. 'Putin', a man of no more than thirty years old liked to drink the Ilocano spirit called *'basi'*[67] early in the morning. He would easily get tipsy, and in that condition, he would wait in the middle of the road for his prey. I was his 'bête noire'[68] and even if I dressed in disguise and stayed away from the road, I was afraid he could smell me.

It was as if I was part of his daily ritual, and he was doing the role of a self-appointed enforcer.

He would look at me menacingly, a five-year-old boy, block my track, point his index finger and say, "Why are you slow, you will be late. You study, study, study. Be a lawyer!" Then he would curse me in Ilocano.

I would run, not turning my head back until I reached school. At first, I was reluctant to go to school again because of him and my mother did not force me to go because I was not really of school age anyhow. But the school appealed to me even then and this feeling overcame my fear of 'Putin'. Later, I would wake up early for school and meet a tiddly 'Putin' by the road as if it has become our ritual. Our conversation, actually a monologue, was enriched from his admonition for studying hard to encouraging me to drink the daily milk rationed by the government for kids in the school. It was a piece of ironic advice from an adult who started the day drinking fermented sugar-cane juice.

The day I did not see him, the trek to school seemed

---

[67] Fermented alcoholic beverage made from sugarcane in the Ilocos region.
[68] A person strongly detested or disliked.

uneventful. I missed his harmless clowning. So, every time I see one who is drunk, I see only the clown in him, my 'Putin'.

Thinking of the psychological scrimmage with 'Putin' and the way I fought my fears at a young age, made me forget my apprehensions of being alone in the city. Since then, many demons had tried to obscure my way and I faced them as I faced 'Putin'.

My fellow passenger, the one who reminded me of 'Putin' woke up sober. He was a student coming back to Manila after a summer break. He had none of the shyness of a provincial lad. He has the slickness of a city boy with the tempting way he talked about pleasure and leisure in Manila. I listened attentively as he ate my bananas one at a time. It did not take long for him to get a good share of the bundle. But Nana Ingga's sweet rice cake was spared for the rest of the trip.

With experience on his side, having been in Manila, this face-off with him was a mismatch. To an adolescent, he could be the dangerous influence of many youthful lives gone sour or a mentor to provide tutorials in adulthood in the long-term or in that immediate now of a boy's provincial life adjusting to city culture.

The passenger bus reached its Sampaloc station in Manila and everyone started to rush to the exit door. The sun was going down fast and turned into the most beautiful sunset in the world. It was starting to grow dark.

"Lakay," [69] he said, "I will wait outside the bus. I am Manny", he introduced himself.

When an Ilocano greets another Ilocano using 'lakay', it

---

[69] Ilocano word for old man but evolved into a word used to call or greet another Ilocano male with fondness.

creates an instant connection, a kinship, regardless of the circumstances and locale, even when they are overseas.

*I will not be alone after all,* I thought with relief. I was gaining confidence to face this uncharted city. I was about to leave my seat, but discovered my left shoe was missing. Just then I remembered removing my shoes when I lay down to sleep. I waited for the passengers to disembark so I could check every corner of the floor for my shoe.

The missing left shoe was stuck in the third row from the driver under the seat near the window. But it took me some time before I saw it and when I finally made it down, the bus had moved around the corner where it was to be parked.

Once I exited the bus, I looked for Manny, but he was gone.

\*

I was not prepared to be alone in the city. Nothing in my young life had prepared me for it. How would I respond to the adversity which is hitherto unknown to a rural boy arriving in a city jungle for the first time?

The warmth of the tears on my cheeks relieved me of my anxieties and the effort to control any sound of crying gave me momentary relief from the fear of the unknown lurking in the chaotic streets of Manila.

A police jeep was parked nearby. Manny was inside the jeep in handcuffs. He could not see me from where he was. A policeman was looking for Manny's 'younger brother', so I heard. This was his claim to the police. I did not know why he was taken into custody.

I remember my mother giving me a piece of paper. I

looked for it inside my pants. It was there with the money sewn in my front-right pants pocket. It was an address and a direction.

My bag was light. Just a few pieces of old hand-me-down shirts, three pairs of underwear, and a pair of black pants. This was the entire universe of my possessions. I sat on one of the benches in the bus station, ate my sweet rice cake, and drank my water. This meal served as my lunch, snack, and early dinner. I also composed myself to plan my next move. This initiated me in the habit of pausing, taking stock of the situation before making a crucial move.

The direction was accurate but the way there shocked me. I passed by a road with an 'estero' on the side. There were a lot of makeshift houses on the way, the informal settlers of Manila.

I felt compassion for those living in such low circumstance, yet the emotion brought my spirits up, like wings to raise me above my pitiful life. I recalled my father telling me about people without shoes whenever I complained about my old ones.

I was a thousand kilometres away from home and just about twelve hours since I left. It was night-time in an unfamiliar place, a city that was dangerous for a rural teen.

The alley was dark, and the air was stale. So is the future. Now that I sensed reality it gave me the creeps that my escape was headlong to hell.

A fool's errand for the boy who did not listen to his father.

# 4
# FLUTTER OF A BUTTERFLY WING

Pliny the Elder[70] who lived from 23 to 79 A.D., had once said that 'God has no power over the past except to cover it with oblivion'. But on my first morning in Manila, Pliny's remarks had taken a new context.

I thought that the darkness of the previous night was not God's gloomy welcome but his mercy to cover my eyes on my first few hours in the city from the ugliness of the urban squalor where I found myself.

The shadows of makeshift houses along the estero[71] on my way to the boarding house the night before came alive with people living in filth but otherwise chattering happily that another day had passed and a new one had arrived.

The idle talk was a resignation to hopelessness, I thought.

It reminded me of the scenes in Victor Hugo's *Les Misérables*, a book I reviewed as student for my literature subject at the community college in Santiago. While Hugo's poor characters took the streets against their king, I was walking along the estero to a university to seek knowledge!

---

[70] Roman author who wrote the ENCYLOPEDIC NATURALIS HISTORIA, which became an editorial model for encyclopedias.
[71] Canal filled with dirty water and garbage.

I wondered if these people would leave Manila for a better life in the province. I wished, if so, that the slow and serene life in a rural area like Santiago would make them intuitive beyond their five senses and that as a result would inform them of the meaning and direction they needed in life.

With these reflections, the clash of wills between my father and mother the night of my escape has a contrasting quality. My father may have wanted to spare me from living in a chaotic and unforgiving circumstance or my mother had willed for me to taste the experience in the city and learn from it meaningfully. To her, this misery is not imagined but real, she having lived in Manila in 1939, where she worked as a sales assistant for a Chinese merchandising store in the Divisoria district to earn additional income for her family back in Pangasinan. For my father, his own experience tells him there is virtue in the calmness of his household steeped in Christian values.

The issue debated in my father's genteel household that night in 1962 had defined the life of their son and shaped his ideas, character and beliefs. From the dust of the events that followed, I emerged a stranger to my parents and those around me.

Is this how the human species, the homo sapiens, transcended the different stages of evolution, where choices are made, and reactions are called for when their existence is challenged? With our will or by pure chance, we survived to a higher level and in gradual progression, we reached this stage of development.

I felt like I was an example in that human struggle. Or, that I am a character in a Greek drama left alone in the wild to fend for himself while the Gods are betting against each other whether I will survive or how long I will last.

To a sixteen-year-old kid who wants to study in Manila, this episode is momentous. But decades later looking back to this day with my head in the clouds, the decision that night and the miserable surroundings I found myself the following day, it could have been far-fetched to imagine how my role was consequential in the events that unfolded many decades later. But not if education and experience, both fountains of wisdom, will be considered in the equation.

To add a romantic adventure to it, I was like a "flutter of a butterfly wing" with a future ripple effect.

A year earlier in 1961 marked the election of Diosdado Macapagal[72] dubbed the poor boy from the town of Lubao in the Province of Pampanga in Central Luzon, as president of the Philippines. Twenty-six years later, in 1998, his daughter Gloria Macapagal-Arroyo[73] will be elected vice president to a popular movie actor, Joseph Ejercito Estrada. [74]

After three years, President Estrada will be ousted in the second people power revolution in the Philippines after an aborted impeachment trial in the Senate.

The succession of Diosdado's daughter as president was a cruel twist of political fortune for Estrada whose roles in the movies as jeepney driver, local hood or farm help made him hugely popular among the Filipino masses while Gloria, the petite and talented economics professor did not have the semblance of charisma at all.

---

[72] 9th President of the Philippines (1961 – 1965)
[73] 14th President of the Philippines (2001 – 2010).
[74] 13th President of the Philippines (1998 – 2001).

*

That night, there is no portent of that future scenario. Instead, a morality drama played out without any audience to applaud or to judge. A young lad's future was on balance in a neutral zone: a bedroom.

The setting is quaint, but it had the intensity of emotions, like a great battlefield. It is where life is formed but likewise, where many lives are destroyed in a burst of emotions. A theatre, a stage, a dome, you name it, a bedroom is as much a place where countless plots of moral dimension take place.

Borrowing from a Greek metaphor, fate may have been there in disguise. Perhaps that night she was the ember of light that illuminated the tears on my mother's face.

Fate visits the lives of people both the great and the simple. The Greeks of antiquity dramatised fate as 'Gods playing favourites' among men, and their stories, when understood behind the allegory, can guide us to deal with our own fates. The monument to the ancient Greeks' folly on fate is the Oracle of Delphi[75] whose God, Apollo, spoke through his priestess Pythia, with an obscure and ambiguous response to the people's query. These are interpreted by the priests of the temple. Since they knew geopolitics, the relationship about kings during their time, well-informed of the balance of power around them, they gave an educated guess when consulted whether to go to war or not.

But the temple priest's advice gave enough leeway to exercise free will. With time, a debate raged among them as to

---

[75] Delphi was considered to be the centre of the world and the Oracle was the most important shrine in all Greece.

which of the contrasting concepts of will or fate determine the outcome of human and state affairs.

The will-and-fate dichotomy, to my mind, are best illustrated by the disparate forces that ignited the French revolution. A choice was made by Louis XVI in 1775 to inaugurate his coronation to the throne of France with pomp and pageantry to remind the French people of the divinity of his kingship. Perhaps his main adviser, the clergy, had wished to shoot two birds with one stone; the other bird was to reinforce the notion that behind the divinity of the king is the divinity of the Church.

It was a decision which he and the clergy would soon regret. For on the day of his coronation, a fifteen-year-old George-Jacques Danton — a boy of poor means but middle-class taste of education — travelled to Paris and patiently waited to see the new king emerge from the coronation. He expected to be enchanted but instead saw a boy made ordinary by the outsized pageantry. The pomp even diminished the monarchy in his eyes. With the bankruptcy of the French coffers many years later, the king was forced to convene the Estate General, an assembly consisting of the nobility, the clergy, and the commoners, the latter being the sole taxpayers. The king's weakness showed him begging for funds from his subjects who were justifiably infuriated by carrying the burden of spending for the lavish court while the clergy and the nobility remained exempt from paying taxes. Danton, who was then a lawyer and with the confidence of an officer of the king's court, became the firebrand that sent the ordinary French marching to the Bastille under the cries of liberty, equality, fraternity or death. The crescendo of the outcry of the

'Les Misérables'[76] ended with the abolition of the monarchy and the establishment of the French republic.

The unstoppable force that toppled the monarchy was the result of individual acts wilfully and knowingly pursued but no one man had planned or consciously willed the fate that eventually followed. It was tragic and bloody with Louis XVI losing his head in the guillotine in 1793, eighteen years after his inauguration as king. When he died the French saw him not as their king but an ordinary man with ordinary clothes and ordinary name, Louis Capet.

The different acts that preceded the French revolution came from the individual. It was the decisions made by Louis XVI and Danton, along with a host of other likeminded people who braved the cannons and bayonets of the loyal palace guards, during the French Revolution, that set in motion everything that followed. But it is the overwhelming force of these actions that fuelled the downfall of the most durable monarchy in Europe at that time and the founding of the French Republic where the power shifted to the people. Fate is not a conscious effort but a zeitgeist that changes the world order.

In the case of the ousted President 'Erap'[77] Estrada, his weaknesses may have brought him in the crosshairs of fate, consolidating a process which commenced in the year 2000 when a former senator and an incumbent representative of congress called me to prepare a complaint of impeachment. The filing of that impeachment complaint in the House of Representatives; his trial in the Senate; a fatal vote against the

---

[76] The destitute or the wretched poor.

[77] Filipino moniker inverted from the word 'pare' or buddy.

opening of an envelope allegedly containing explosive and incriminating evidence; a walkout, and military and civilian withdrawal of support completed the mix that led to his ouster.

Of course, all these slides would not become apparent until years later.

*

It was summer and a full moon. There was a soft breeze coming from the mountains. The noises of the boys playing outside mixed with the sound of a nightingale. A beautiful song from a small bird soothes tired souls. Rural life is simple but rich in things without material value.

"I cannot afford to send him to a university in Manila," I heard my father say with final resignation.

"He can remain here, finish his two-year college course and then work. He is comfortable here, eats three times a day."

I could feel the hardwood floor on the second floor where we were staying tremble as if telling me that a banquet at home is a future ruin in disguise. There is only the '*banig*' made of abaca fibre, laid on the floor every night, rolled into a tube and stocked behind a wooden unattached cabinet, the '*aparador*', [78] every morning, that protects my back.

I never felt impoverished by that. Perhaps it is because I have never seen the life of another boy more comfortable than my lot. Ignorance is really bliss. Despite the austere conditions, honour, and dignity dominated my father's home. If I felt a high sense of dignity even under humble circumstances throughout my life, it is the legacy of that

---

[78] Unattached wooden clothes closet usually with a long mirror.

household and the way my father presided at the family meals. There is another reason for his objection. He knew I had a curious mind. 'Curiosity kills the cat,' he always warned me with care. To him, I can be vulnerable to different ideas apart from what he believed in when exposed to new surroundings. What he feared most is a door would be opened to a new belief system in my relations with God, and who He is.

*

At my age, my father had already suffered sorrows and life's unbearable blows. Now, wanting to protect his son, the sad memories returned.

He was seventeen years old when he joined a band of men roaming in the countryside not as brigands but preaching a new kind of interpretation of the gospel of Jesus. They were reminiscent of the gyrovagues[79] of the early faithful in Europe as the Christian church was starting to grow.

Individually, these men were scarcely educated, no pedigrees, no outstanding achievements, not a book written or contributed any invention, but inspired by their repeated reading of the scriptures. Starting as a ragtag of a few men, they became an army that changed people's attitudes, blunted the horns of the criminally inclined and redirected the superstitious tendencies of the weak.

Their leader and founder, Felix Manalo,[80] who had been born a Catholic, had joined many Christian denominations,

---

[79] Wandering preachers.
[80] He registered the sect in the Philippines on July 27, 1914, and was its first Executive Minister.

foremost of which is the Seventh-day Adventists[81] before he started his church in 1914. He called it *Iglesia Ni Cristo*. He claims to be the last messenger of God because he saw signs that it is already the end of the world in fulfilment of a prophecy.

When these few itinerant biblical preachers were welcomed to their house in Urdaneta, Pangasinan, to stay for the night, my father was already a battle-scarred seventeen-year-old man, both physically and mentally. His curious mind, his sense of adventure and his restless soul had nowhere to go, and a vacuum was created as the *colorums* which he had earlier joined had capitulated to the government troops. It left him a heart boiling with disappointment, hopelessness, turning into hatred which could be deadly to his well-being, making him socially unfriendly and unhappy, if not eased, before it reaches a tipping point.

When he heard these men sing, pray, and preach from their hearts, a key inside him turned to open and release those pent-up emotions and tamed the aggression within himself. His observant sister whose sincere piety made her spiritually sensitive saw this as a transforming force such that she set aside her own religious preferences to make these strangers comfortable in their home. Before the week was over, his sister lost my father to a cult and her welcome to this group turned into an annoyance. However, she accepted this with reluctance as a better alternative to a life of a restless rebel and fugitive brother. Soon, she could not bear this ideological distance with her brother and rather than hurt him with the intolerant

---

[81] Protestant Christian denomination distinguished by its observance of Saturday.

treatment, she got married and followed the lure of a promise of a new life in Mindanao.[82] The brother and sister never saw each other again. All these personal experiences, rather than being embittering, appealed to the kinder side of my father's personal growth that readied him for a spiritual life.

*

My mother was industrious. She would travel from Santiago, Isabela to Bangar, La Union, a town with native textile industry, to buy wholesale the famous *'abel'*.[83]

Santiago, Isabela is part of a valley that is a breadbasket for *palay*, [84] corn, tobacco and the places near the Pacific coastline are teeming with timber and bountiful with fruit-bearing trees.

The valley is a melting pot but mostly from the hardworking Ilocanos coming from the western coastal provinces of Luzon, such as Pangasinan, La Union, and Ilocos. Ilocanos are hardy people, ambitious, education-oriented and are attached to where they began. But they were practical people and would not hesitate to leave their places of origin to move to other places where they can have a better life.

The diaspora of the Ilocanos made the provinces of the north of Manila practically their homeland. In the Philippine political narrative, it is referred to as the 'solid north'. However, to the Ilocanos living outside the big swathe of land, the solid north is in the mind. They are everywhere, in Manila,

---

[82] Common name when referring to southern Philippines; 3rd largest island of the country.

[83] Famous Ilocos fabric known for its durability and strength.

[84] Rice that has not been husked.

Mindanao, Hawaii, the mainland United States. They all belong to the 'solid north'. In Philippine politics, the 'solid north' has always been an enigma. It is a prize to be won by any presidential candidate.

My mother would go to the town of Bangar over and over again against all the risks. It took two days for her to get there.

The road is dangerous and the only access to the lowland from the valley is through the Dalton Pass at Santa Fe, Province of Nueva Vizcaya. Otherwise, you go further north to Cagayan and pass that Patapat Road on the northernmost tip of Luzon to go to the Ilocos. It was a longer route and equally dangerous.

It was just more than a decade after World War II and Dalton Pass was mentioned prominently as one of the escape routes of Japan's Yamashita, the 'Butcher of Malaya'. It was a natural terrain for the bandits to conduct their hijacks and for the anti-government *'hukbalahap'* [85] to ambush military convoys. The *hukbalahaps* were a potent and heroic guerrilla force against the Japanese occupiers in World War II.

To keep the citizens safe from the bandits and the insurgents, the military ordered a convoy from the outskirts of Cordon at specific hours. These convoys are long queue of public and private vehicles, sometimes as long as two kilometres as they navigate the uphill and downhill road to Nueva Vizcaya town of Solano[86] where another convoy starts in the counter direction towards Isabela. The same pattern takes place from the Dalton Pass until the first town of Nueva

---

[85] A derivative of "Hukbong Laban sa Hapon', an anti-Japanese army formed by farmers with socialist/communist leanings.
[86] Third-class municipality of Isabela near to the City of Santiago.

Ecija, which tells you that you are already in the central plain provinces. These convoys added to the travel time.

This was the late 1950s.

Despite her modest income, my mother kept a spartan household. Boiled green vegetables from the garden and dried salted fish from the lowlands. The big fresh waters of the valley provided cheap good protein. Once a week, usually Saturdays, we feasted with *'pinapaitan'*, a popular Ilocano food which has goat meat as its principal ingredient.

*

'Nanang' as I called my mother, was my first teacher and her stories helped the development of my character and creative mind. My first classroom was her bedroom where she read to me the Ilocano magazine *Bannawag*. She would be unpredictable by deviating from the stories. She always added to the plot making me the character in a starring role. She painted our study rituals with a lively and dreamy palate, predicting my future as either a doctor, an engineer, or lawyer, but no matter what, she always emphasised that I would be a successful family man with children so she could dote on them as a grandmother. She was in a great hurry to see me succeed.

When my mother was in her nineties, she would wait for me so we could eat breakfast together, just the two of us. I sensed that she was waiting for me to tell her stories about anything, in my work, my sons, about events, the latest news. I now realise that those times with me were her reason to live another day.

But I had come close to see a preview of how she dealt with problems. During one of our breakfasts, I thought of writing her story in her own words. She was regaling me with stories about her great-grandfathers and how her father met her mother. It was how she faced the Japanese soldiers during World War II that revealed her strong character. The Japanese soldiers were approaching the place where they were hiding, and she could see the atrocities being committed. They were getting nearer and came dangerously almost face to face. She was looking at them, her mind saying that her God is more powerful and willed that they cannot prevail. Then she closed her eyes to wait for the next act, a sound of rifle fire or the pain from a bayonet thrust, but the Japanese soldiers stopped what they were doing and left. She said she had an anticipatory feeling of the turn of events. She was unbowed.

I was fortunate to have written the story down and I still have the four pages which contained a compressed memoir of her life. There were not many details in it, but you can safely infer a colourful and complete picture of her dramatic life. Great men usually leave memoirs of hundreds of pages, but this four-page memoir was enough to formalise her greatness in my mind.

*

The drift of my mother's thoughts was to hold her ground which is an act of defiance to which she is unaccustomed. She was waiting for a hint from heaven, but it seems that fate itself refused to intervene. The risk of possible ruin of her son in an unaided life in the city would be her sole responsibility, a burden she had usually shared with her husband.

Her own experience with her brother's education flashed back to her like a recorded memory. Her family was likewise confronted with the decision to send their only brother to the premier state-run agricultural high school in Central Luzon for his studies. This required all the financial resources of the family and to deprive her and the five other siblings, all girls, of their own formal education. But she rallied her siblings to this singular cause, and they even worked to contribute to the needs of her brother who eventually finished a fine high school education. It was not lost to her however that she and her siblings borne too much responsibility for their brother who squandered the chance to develop a strong will and character because of the ease and comfort provided by his adoring sisters. She knew she had committed a mistake!

She wanted to be right this time for her son.

For my father, this is the innocence of life that is worth preserving. He values peace of mind. His philosophy: God provides! He knows your needs!

My mother, however, saw the real world, a bigger world. She saw it in her travels from Santiago to the Ilocos. Having food on the table blindsides the reality of a future of want and hopelessness. Her travels gave her a peek of the world in all its imperfections and worries. One must act now to provide for the future.

For my father, a simple prayer suffices. My mother had the iron will. They clash about my education from those standpoints.

It is a classic debate. I see the artistry in this life's play, a silent duel of parental wisdom taking place. Fate may have been smiling watching *noblesse oblige* [87] among ordinary

---

[87] The inferred responsibility of privileged people to act with generosity and nobility toward those less privileged.

mortals.

For the first time in her married life, she disobeyed my father's decision. She opened her bamboo coin bank, pulled some money from under some folded clothes and from under the bed too, and I had enough for my transportation and two months' stay in Manila which she stitched into my pants where it would be safe. She knows.

She was not asking me to jump from the perch of a high tree. She was pushing me to the river with a makeshift raft to hold onto. A bone may be broken but it will heal in time.

But she wanted an insurance and that was God's protection. To her, I will always be safe if I stick to the sect's religious practices. She made me vow to continue with my faith in God by attending religious services every Thursday and Sunday which our sect dictated.

Before the night was over, the conspiracy of the mother and son was sealed. While my father slept soundly at dawn, I escaped!

This was my first journey to the city alone.

Was it fate or the strong will of my mother that my flight from home contributed about four decades later in 2001 to the downfall of a popular president and other acts that influenced the election of another president in 2016?

If I were a butterfly, my mother was the wind that made me flutter.

# 5

# QUIAPO

In my first two months in Manila, I stayed in a small open room hanging under the stairs. I learnt to match footsteps to the owners' feet. I came to know who was going up or down. I could tell if it's the lady bed spacer, [88] or the young student, or the lady housecleaner. When the footsteps were heavy, the owner dragging his feet as if intentionally creating the noise to irritate me, I knew it was the guy who pays for his lease by subleasing small bed spaces.

The experience taught me empathy with those who were at the bottom of the food chain as I have experienced. I appreciate the footsteps of 'Manang', [89] our cleaner, who took the stairs almost without any noise. It's ironic that the unschooled among us in that apartment was the one conscious of someone resting from a day's work under the stairs.

Later, whenever I look at the stairs with a little room under it, I remember ample lessons in life such as compassion, humility, weighing the best options, fighting for the right.

Changing my lodging meant additional financial burden. Since the new place was better with my own bed, I was required to put down a month's deposit which I did not have.

---

[88] A renter of any floor area used for sleeping.
[89] Older sister as a respect.

I begged the landlady to accept a partial deposit, the money from Manny, as I was waiting for my allowance from home. She bought the lie.

My finances were short but my dreams were not short-sighted. I saw the road ahead of me in the next five years. I hope to complete my pre-law course with five semesters left for a Bachelor's Degree in Arts. Then I will move forward for a law degree. In six years at the age of twenty-four, I will be a lawyer. I saw myself with a big briefcase like those lawyers I saw talking with my father.

*

With no money, I walked to downtown Quiapo[90] looking for a job.

Quiapo was the centre of life for students of the university belt. There is anachronism in the set-up where history clashes with the present. While Quiapo became a seat of learning being the host to the university belt, it is also where the centuries-old Quiapo church is. This is the home of the Black Nazarene which draws millions of devotees in a single day of religious procession called *'Traslación'*[91] on the ninth of January to commemorate the arrival of the image in Manila from Mexico. The religious fanatics believe miracles of cure and riches by mere touching of the image during that day. The students in the university belt were largely noncommittal about participating in the frenzy of devotion and would prefer to touch their books that teach logic and science. Despite their

---

[90] A district in the City of Manila, in the National Capital Region.
[91] Catholic procession moving the Nazarene from one place to another.

ambivalence to what the religious practice around the Black Nazarene[92] can bring to a devotees' life, the students remained respectful and tolerant of centuries of tradition. The Black Nazarene had a life of its own in the psyche of students who, after years of reason and science, still make homage to that piece of furniture or what it represents to pray on Sundays, to pass the bar or licensure examinations. After reason, there is a tendency of human nature to seek the safety net of faith!

I saw one notice of a vacancy for a typist. Those days the typewriter was mechanical and the Underwood[93] was state of the art. When an error in typing was committed, you had to retype the page or make a careful erasure. Later, there was what was called *'snopake'*, correction fluid.

Passing the job test, I started working with an empty stomach. My employer liked my work. While typing fast, I was also correcting the grammar and spelling of the manuscripts at the same time. These were term papers submitted by students in their history or political science subjects. I am sure they got better grades due to my corrections.

There was double compensation, one in non-material way. I learnt a lot while typing their research. There are always additional benefits in anything you do. Walking in the park, for example, is not just exercise. You can learn that there are smart plants that reach upward to meet the sunlight.

'To read is to lead', is something I read in one of the papers. Here is knowledge stocked in my mind which later

---

[92] Life-sized image of a dark-skinned kneeling Jesus Christ carrying the cross.

[93] A known brand of typewriter.

gave me the confidence to express my ideas. At the canteen, my friends were surprised at my contribution to new discoveries and new thoughts.

I was happy to share my experience and the knowledge learnt with my colleagues at the canteen. One evening, I posed as a challenge to interpret a poem from Emily Dickenson[94] lifted from one of the term papers I was typing:

"I took my power in my hand
And went against the world;
'Twas not so much as David had,
But I was twice as bold.
I aimed my pebble, but myself
Was all the one that fell.
Was it Goliath was too large,
Or only I too small?"

Sooner than I finished the last word when a torrent of dialectic broke out about the relevance of our education for our future.

Mr Hot Head, who was able to inch back to the group, was there but this time more subdued and contented as listening post than an active participant. We received him guardedly and all eyes managed to conceal that he was under observation. He did well. This time around he showed more regard to everybody especially to me. He has learnt to banter lightly and devoid of casuistry. The experience which bloodied me had made him a changed man. I was particularly elated that I had shown the other cheek to his erstwhile violence.

"Our little learning may be dangerous to us in the end. We can be bold yet still small in our knowledge!"

---

[94] One of America's greatest and most original poets of all time.

"But it is not enough that we gain knowledge. We must learn history as well, what we are and why we are that we became what we are?"

A pre-law student cited that the United States still allows racial discrimination after more than one hundred years since their civil war.

"The blacks are bold, even bolder than David, but racism was too large, it was their Goliath!" The comment came from Clyde, a history student, a Filipino with a black complexion. His father was a black US serviceman. He came from Olongapo City where Subic Bay, the home of the US Naval Base, was located.

· He narrated that long after the establishment of Harvard University, slaves were still sold in Virginia. He pulled a piece of typewritten paper from his wallet about the sale of land and other property, near Petersburg, Virginia. He begun to read a portion:

*"We xxx unexpectedly saw slaves sold at public auction. Xxx A white boy, about fifteen years old, was placed on the stand. His hair was brown and straight, his skin exactly the same hue as other white person's, and no discernible trace of negro features in his countenance."*

We were all surprised about a white boy being a slave when we thought that slavery was all about the blacks. But we allowed him to continue as this is a new piece of information and we wanted to expand our take on American history of slavery.

He continued reading:

"Some said a white nigger was more trouble than he was worth. One man said it was wrong to sell white people. I asked him if it was more wrong than to sell black people. He made no reply. Before he was sold, his mother rushed from the house upon the portico, crying, in frantic grief, 'My son, O! my boy, they will take away my dear—' Her voice was lost, as she was rudely pushed back, and the door closed. The sale was not for a moment interrupted, and none of the crowd appeared to be in the least affected by the scene. The poor boy, afraid to cry before so many strangers, who showed no signs of sympathy or pity, trembled and wiped the tears from his cheeks with his sleeves. He was sold for about two hundred fifty dollars."[95]

If the sale of people is brutal enough, the punishment of slaves was horrifying. Clyde related the story of a black woman who had been stripped entirely naked and strapped to a tree being lashed with a long whip, while strip after strip of skin peeled off, "gash after gash was cut in her living flesh, until it became livid and bloody mass of raw and quivering muscle." Samuel Gridley Howe, [96] an author, and a leading American educator, in his eyewitness account remarked that "so low can man, created in God's image, be sunk in brutality".

I asked about the piece of paper containing the story and he said that he will keep it as long as it takes to redeem the American black.

Someone dismissed the story as history and no longer relevant and said that we should move on. I felt it was insensitive to leave the narration without any closure. Clyde insisted that there is still slavery in the south of the United

---

[95] American Slavery: Sale of Slaves, Virginia, December 1846 by Dr. Elwood Harvey.

[96] A noted philanthropist and physician, and an advocate of abolishing slavery.

States even after the so-called emancipation of the slaves by Abraham Lincoln and it is in a different form which is more psychological but equally demeaning with the blind eye of the US Congress and the US Supreme Court. That is why they have the euphemistic equal-but-separate doctrine that justified the policy of segregation in the southern states which mandated separate public places and transport between blacks and whites.

Our discussion took place one or two years before the assassination of Martin Luther King who advocated the integration of the races to attain equality.

We complimented Clyde for his contribution and after a few seconds of shocked silence, another student changed the conversation by pointing out that our immediate concern must be our own version of 'slavery' to ignorance and dependence or lack of self-reliance.

"We are also in the dark because of ignorance and dependence or lack of self-reliance. It makes us small against our challenges, against our Goliath."

"My mother is a slave for all intents and purposes to pay for the loan she got for my trip to Manila!" Another student decried his mother sinking low to give him access to education. "If we do not watch out," he said, "those vices will lead us to the selling of our own patrimony and even our political independence."

"Let us gather pebbles of knowledge and the emphasis must be on technology. The Japanese are small people, but no problem is too large for them because of their technology. That is why they have easily recovered after the war."

The remark came from a student pursuing a Master's degree in education.

Another history student butted in: "Do not forget the Marshall Plan of the United States.[97] Germany's education and culture and the Marshall Aid got them back on their feet after the war. It was the shining glory of the United States to bring prosperity back to Europe and the world. A country may have its plusses and minuses."

We all concluded that we need education, technology, and money. These must be our capital, our pebbles.

"Abraham Lincoln[98] did not have much of a degree but he became a good lawyer and great president. Education need not be a paper chase but learning from experience as was his case," another student shared.

The discussion, though undisciplined and disorganise, made us feel free to express many insights which were appreciated. As a result, each of us felt we were getting a good education during our meetings at the canteen.

"I read somewhere that Lincoln married a girl from a prominent family. Let us all become lawyers and marry rich widows to be prosperous."

We all laughed at the levity mirroring life and when we looked at the guilty party, it was Mr Hot Head.

The canteen talks and my life at work were so intertwined. While I was earning barely enough money for my upkeep, what was more important was that I was also learning important life lessons.

*

---

[97] A European Recovery Program of the US.
[98] 16th President of the US (1861 – 1865) issuing the Emancipation Proclamation that declared the slaves forever free!

The typist I replaced visited me one day. He told me that the purchasing department in a big company in Manila's port area had an opening for a typist. I went to the address, and I was immediately accepted, so I left my first typing job. It was a pleasant parting. The owner praised the work I did and assured me that the door was always open if I decided to return. It boosted my self-esteem by going to the next job.

I thought the new job was a done deal. But it did not happen the way I expected. There is competition for work even at that level. The head of the medical department had a daughter who married a bum. The doctor wanted his daughter's husband to be employed so he asked the head of the purchasing department to hire him. The doctor was a close friend of a top company executive who was in charge of the treasury and the purchasing department was under the treasury.

My resume was not impressive but I was the best typist so I assured myself he could not tear my skill away. The head of the purchasing department was a fair guy and had already committed to hiring me before the bum came into the picture.

The company was at the port area and would require me to travel in passenger jeepneys daily to Quiapo to catch up with my evening class. The business of the company was lighterage and salvage operation. It operated many tugboats and barges. The purchasing department was always busy buying parts that are all urgently needed for the operation. As a requirement, the purchases must be justified by a purchase order and to prepare a purchase order, it needed many signatures from the end-user up to the treasury department. It entailed a lot of time to secure, and tugboats cannot wait. To respond quickly, they use old, unused purchase orders. It was to be my job to look for these purchase orders. This requires patience and also fast typing. Mr Richie Boy did not have either patience or skill. But he had his father-in-law.

The purchasing manager was in a serious predicament.

As expected, the doctor had his way. His son-in-law was hired as a regular employee. I did not insist because all I needed was some extra money for my room and board. My priority was to finish my pre-law course studies and after that, go to law school.

The purchasing head hired me nevertheless, but my pay would come from his own funds. I received an allowance at the end of the week, on Saturdays. I did not have any security of tenure, no social security protection or any company benefits. Officially, I did not exist on the roster of employees.

I was grateful for his generosity. When I became a lawyer of the U.S. Naval Base of the Seventh Fleet[99] in Subic Bay, his son had grown up and became a businessman. He came to my office for advice. I did not hesitate to guide and help him with his business problem.

The purchasing department had accredited regular suppliers and agents who gave priority to produce the needs for emergency spare parts on a commission basis for the company. Sometimes they would deliver the spare parts without the necessary purchase orders because of the urgency of the repair works. They would then pressure me to look for old purchase orders from a mountain of files so that their deliveries could be properly documented, and they can get

---

[99] Largest of the US Navy's forward-deployed fleets, where at any given time there were roughly 50-70 ships and submarines, 140 aircraft and approximately 20,000 sailors.

paid for their commissions. The office was festive every Friday when the purchasers or buyers received their commissions. They also gave me and Mr Richie tokens of appreciation.

Soon, Mr Richie Boy was also helping to rummage into the files of purchase orders. The preparation of purchase orders became faster to the delight of the purchasers and suppliers. The purchasers also gave him tokens in cash which gave him the passion to work harder. He became more positive in his attitude in life.

Then, we became friends. He covered for me when I was late or absent during school examinations. Later, after I left the job, he himself went into business. He prospered, to the delight of his father-in-law.

I have always reflected on him and regretted prematurely thinking of him as a bum. Given the right opportunity and incentive, a person can change for the better. It takes a push for a person to take the right path. In his case, it was his father-in-law. Of course, the father-in-law did not do it for him, he did it for his beloved daughter.

I thought of my father and my mother who debated on the path I had to take that night. My mother's decisive action opened a new world of possibilities to me. She may have known that the world is full of good Samaritans who would negate my father's worst fears. On top of that, the experience enriched his son's humanity and taught him to be a good Samaritan himself.

# 6
# WHIRLPOOL IN PORT AREA

It was not long before I realised that our canteen was merely the initial stage where young boys learnt to interact in the real world. We had yet to get our feet immersed in an uncontrolled setting. In my case, the canteen was an ideal spot for a rural kid to start developing a new behaviour and cultural taste requisite in a city. It was not the testing ground.

Instead, working at the port area was going deeper into the whirlpool of the capital city, where the untested lad would face the brute forces of a so-called melting pot. It is where a strict taskmaster lays down a crash course on how to deal with day-to-day life. To paraphrase a song in eisegesis, *'if you can make it in Manila, you can make it anywhere'*.[100]

Nothing had prepared me for the actual challenges of a workplace. So far, my young mind was titillated by Tata Abon's fables where problems are overcome by making the impossible possible. Tata Abon's method was easy. I had control of the imagined dangers which I could add to or subtract from. It was limitless as far as I could perceive, and devoid of stress because of the expediency of flight from the difficulties.

But the reality of a working place poses challenges over

---

[100] Interpretation of a text.

which you do not have control. Once set in motion, the choices are limited. No one teaches you how to deal with it. The lesson comes after the test; an acid test that one must endure.

It was another step on the staircase of my experience.

*

It came one Friday afternoon at about four o'clock. I was preparing to leave the purchasing office when a notice came from the legal department of the company. It said that I will have to report to them the following Monday at ten o'clock in the morning. My pass to enter the company compound the following day, Saturday, was cancelled.

Could this be connected to the incident that morning when the purchasing manager was asked to take his leave of absence?

I had not received my allowance yet which was due the following day. They said it will be given to me the following Monday. It turned out that all payments of purchases were suspended. We were all penniless going into the weekend.

I arrived at the school earlier than usual. A friend told me that someone would like to meet me at the canteen. The man, in his late thirties, was in a black blazer with denim pants and shiny leather shoes. He was with two men who kept a distance from us.

He greeted me in Ilocano.

"How are you doing with your studies?"

"I am good sir. It is hard but I am not complaining."

"You have good grades according to the dean. You only paid half your tuition for two semesters."

"It was partial scholarship," I said. "If I were not working,

I could do full," I murmured to myself lest he find me boastful.

*The guy is thorough,* I thought. He had done a background check on me and I wondered if he might offer me a job.

He ordered good food for us. When a student played the jukebox, he motioned one of his guys to stop it. He knew how to assert power.

"Some people are framing our candidate for president, our fellow Ilocano," he said appealing to my regional bias for his candidate. "There are tires purchased by the company you worked for, and they are saying these were installed on his car. It is untrue!" he clarified.

*This is big time,* I told myself. I became flotsam, [101] caught in the political cross-currents of a presidential campaign.

"I don't recall typing a P.O. for car tires. All that we purchased are grey marine engines and items for repair for the barges and tugboats," I said. I talked like I knew my job. Now, I realised the importance of purchase orders.

"Just tell the truth and nothing else." He felt relieved that I did not recall any purchase orders for the tires.

"You are young. Be alert with their questions. It could be a trap and they will use it against our candidate."

Now, I am part of his team.

"I was also a working student like you. Life is hard now, but your experience is only shared by a rare breed. Be strong, have patience, be resilient."

Instantly, we have an affinity.

"You are a brand plucked from the fire," he said with all emotions behind a powerful rhetoric. It is hard for me to hide the pride I felt on hearing those words. A young pre-law

---

[101] Floating debris

student completely won over by a consummate politician and lawyer.

"We will meet again after our candidate wins. Surely, he will win. Just come to me."

His promise was like a dangling carrot, and it gave this struggling student hope.

"Do you see some Americans working there? They are CIA agents. They are part of the scheme working to defeat our candidate. They don't want the country to be independent. Be careful, you could be collateral damage," he said.

He was tense when he talked about the CIA. But he did not elaborate further. My friends were at the other table reading their notes, but I knew they were curious about what we were discussing.

That was the first time I'd heard of the CIA. I worried about his mention of collateral damage. My experience as a young lad from the province had not reached that level of understanding. My imagination was fired up and my curiosity kindled.

I was also scared. Feeling important and frightened when mixed create a profound change in a person's bearing.

I felt tall in front of my friends.

*

It did not take a second after he left that my friends joined me at the table.

I am no longer a mere number to them since my handling of the police investigation at the hospital. I covered for them then and they were very grateful. Mr Hot Head was suspended for a semester but did not come back to our school. Once in a while, he would visit to say hello.

I saw Manny at the door and excused myself from my friends. He said he knew the guy I was talking with and wanted some information. I said there is nothing important to report. He was just visiting me. Manny respected that and moved to leave. "Manny," I said. With my hands stretched out like they were in handcuffs, I asked: "What happened the last time I saw you at the bus station?"

"Next time," he said. "It's a long story." And he left. His body language showed that the incident at the bus station when we arrived in Manila was inconsequential.

My friends were silent and impatient to hear what I had to say. How do I start?

I have learnt a lot about this group. They are well-read but as young students they wanted a life of adventure and there is this possibility waiting to happen. That conspiracy stuff tickles their imagination no end.

"The CIA does not want his candidate for president," I said.

The room came alive with partisan sentiments.

"I like Marcos," said a student from my solid north.

At one time we went together to the Senate on Taft Avenue to watch the session. We heard Marcos speak with eloquence and we were mesmerised by the debates between him and Tolentino[102] and Tañada, [103] two of the respected senators of that era.

---

[102] Senator Arturo Tolentino was a prominent Filipino politician and diplomat who served as Senate President and Secretary of Foreign Affairs.
[103] Senator Lorenzo Tañada was a known oppositionist to martial law under Marcos and to the continued presence of American military bases in the Philippines.

"He is a nationalist, and he wants the US bases to be removed," said one who is a member of an activist student organisation.

"The US bases are here to protect us."

"No, it is actually a magnet for invasion. The US bases will be the first target in case of war. Without the bases, there is no aggression in an empty space. Nagasaki was chosen for the atomic bomb because the place hosted Japan's industrial complex. Luzon will be wiped off the map like Nagasaki and Hiroshima," [104] Rody from Mindanao commented.

Time proved that Rody was right about the American military bases being a target in case of war. When I was invited to speak before a group of lawyers decades later at the former Clark Air Base, [105] there was news of the capability of the North Koreans to launch a missile that could reach as far as the western coast of the United States. I related to the audience about having worked in the US military base and observed that had the Americans still held on to the bases until now, we would be apprehensive staying in Clark. I told them that this is the power of the empty space which was how I described the idea Rody had articulated during our verbal exchanges in the canteen during the sixties.

"Marcos cannot do anything to remove the bases. It is secured by a treaty that guarantees their use of it for the next hundred years," a pro-American student on G.I. scholarship argued.

---

[104] Two Japanese cities that suffered atomic bombs from the US in August 1945 killing between 129,000 to 226,000 people.

[105] Site of US Air Force Base that helped in the evacuation of Marcos, his family and some cohorts when US President Reagan decided to bring them out of the country during the EDSA revolution.

"At least he could do something to reduce the lease to twenty-five years," a foreign service student commented.

After graduation, this student joined the foreign service and during the negotiation for the reduction of the term of the lease, he was part of those doing the staff work. In my case, a year after passing my bar examinations in 1969, I joined the U.S. Naval Base Law Center as a general attorney for the US military members and their families. It was the height of the Vietnam War which the American soldiers had reluctantly supported. I say 'reluctantly' based on the many US servicemen sharing their feelings against the war with me. Even then, I had hoped that the US would leave its military bases which consisted of a huge tract of lands bigger than Singapore at the centre of the Central Luzon. When the US left, that former military base became a growth catalyst and proved that the US bases were a great obstacle to the development of the country in terms of the economy as well as the basis of dependence that destroyed the Filipino's inner sense. There were also talks that the military installation was one of the reasons the US had interfered in the Philippine election of presidents since Manuel Roxas, the first President of the Republic.

Years later, there were reports that the CIA was involved in toppling the leaders of different countries like Vietnam and Chile and fomenting unrest in many countries where the US had strategic interests like oil in the Middle East. This adds credence to the many speculations about the hand of a foreign power in the assassination of Ninoy Aquino, the husband of Cory Aquino, who succeeded Marcos after a people power revolution in 1986.

Santi, who was a sort of a moderator and the most senior

and well-read of our group, weighed in to inject another aspect of the discussion. He read history in the light of the prevailing philosophy that dominated Europe in the twentieth century. I learnt how a thought could be a seed or a germ that could infect the thinking of people who are civilised and allow them to perpetrate the most inhuman and heinous acts against man.

He started, "You know now why Nagasaki and Hiroshima were bombed but you do not know the kind of people who ordered the bomb to be dropped. It was not only because they wanted to stop the war. The Americans have no qualms about killing thousands of Japanese because they considered them of an inferior race."

"I do not think that is the case."

Another student did not allow this qualm thing to pass. "The feeling of pity for the Japanese came to the mind of the crew of the airplanes dispatched to drop the bombs but thought also of the savagery and stealth of the Japanese in bombing Pearl Harbor and the Death March in Bataan."

Santi allowed that part of his history to be corrected and he continued:

"There are thoughts both in America and Russia that shared Germany's thinking about a superior race and an inferior race. The way the Americans treated the Filipinos from the Spanish-American War to the American occupation and until now is influenced by the superior-race mantra."

"The Darwinian influence," another commented.

It was an interesting twist to the discussion. Santi may have opened a Pandora's box of sorts. He continued that when the Americans colonised the Philippines, they claimed it was

'Manifest Destiny'[106] and a duty to liberate the Filipinos from ignorance and make them capable of self-governance. But those who were sent here as administrators felt that they are the superior race, and we are an inferior race.

Social Darwinism [107] was the prevailing thought in American life at the start of the American occupation in the Philippines. In the World's Fair in 1903 [108] in Saint Louis, Missouri, the idea of white superiority, the crux of social Darwinism philosophy, flourished. In the exhibition of the 'development of man', the Philippine Negrito was described as the missing link among the non-Western people assembled there which included the Zulus from South Africa[109] and the native American Indians (now known as Native Americans, of course). It was followed in the same city by the 1904 Olympic Games that featured an alternative game called 'Anthropology Days, [110] organised by whites, to show the differing fitness of the races of mankind. A Moro[111] from the Philippines who was featured in the alternative game won the javelin.

The first civilian Governor-General of the Philippines was

---

[106] The supposed inevitability of the continued territorial expansion of the territorial boundaries of US westward to the Pacific and beyond.

[107] Social Darwinism has been used to justify imperialism, racism, eugenics and social inequality at various times over the past 150 years.

[108] An International Exposition participated in by more than 60 countries and 43 of the then 45 American states with themes on History, Art, Architecture and Anthropology.

[109] Little black people that belong to tribe.

[110] The competition was designed to test the physical abilities of 'primitive' indigenous people to see how they compared to the white man!

[111] Indigenous people populating the southern Philippines even before the arrival and colonisation by the Spaniards.

William Howard Taft[112] whose thinking was sort of a social Darwinist. When he became the US President in 1909, he refused to follow the example of his predecessor, Theodore Roosevelt, [113] of appointing blacks to a federal position. Eugenics was a strong movement in the US in 1920 and at that time, Leonard Darwin, the son of Charles Darwin, had encouraged the policy that superior people breed more than so-called 'inferior people'. [114]

"In the early years of Americans in the Philippines, the people of the mountain province were declared unfit to drink alcohol. Too racist," Harry, an Igorot [115] scholar bitterly complained.

Santi retorted:

"Darwin's Theory of Evolution [116] fathered social Darwinism which was used to justify the superiority of the Aryan race. It was Nietzsche[117] who was an articulate voice of this type of thinking. Hitler was a product of his influence."

"Survival of the fittest, elimination of the unfit!" Lucas, a student from UP, added.

"This theory of superiority found a soft and fertile ground in the Filipino psyche after more than three centuries of Catholic theology of Jesus' tenet of turning the other cheek which encouraged meekness. The friars threatening us with

---

[112] 27th President of the US (1909 – 1913)

[113] 26th President of the US (1901 — 1909)

[114] Beliefs and practices that aim to improve the genetic quality of a human population.

[115] Indigenous people of the mountain area of northern island of Luzon.

[116] Organisms change over time as a result of changes in heritable physical or behavioral traits.

[117] German philosopher known for his writings on good and evil.

hell made us weak."

"There are no masters if there are no slaves." The student who corrected Santi did not let up.

He added that Americans, like the other Europeans who came to Asia, developed a sense of entitlement with the oriental welcoming attitude. He recalled the British Opium Trade[118] that resulted in the British occupation of Macao and Hong Kong and deprived China of these strategic ports.

The well-intentioned among the colonisers thought that we were limp and weak and that we had to be guided, while our elite, who could have been the first line of defence, allied instead with the colonisers to share power and protect their interests, he added!

"Vintage Nietzsche." A philosophy student who has been reading 19th-century philosophers brought the discussion back to Nietzsche. He said that Nietzsche had nurtured his race's superiority philosophy when he was ill with syphilis.

"Poor Asians, we have been treated as trash because of the influence of a syphilitic philosopher," a Chinese student theorised. He was apparently mad and on the brink of cussing.

The group was enveloped by silence. The thought shocked everybody.

Nietzsche was fifteen years old when Darwin's Theory of Evolution was published in 1859. When he was still sane, he remarked: "Without music, life would be a mistake." I thought that quote from him revealed a fine mind. But his superiority of the race philosophy was an errant note to his great

---

[118] The traffic that developed in 18th & 19th centuries in which western countries mostly Great Britain exported opium grown in India and sold it to China.

philosophical mind.

I realised that Nietzsche did not follow what he preached about music. The discordant note created by his thoughts was the eerie sound of dying in the holocaust in World War II. He did not comprehend that the evolution of mankind is like a symphony made of soft human instruments and strong human chords. Without soft instruments as well as strong chords, and notes of equal strength, no good music could be produced.

"How dare he contradict the beautiful human symphony composed by the highest conductor of life?" Rody waxed righteous indignation.

We were worried that he might accidentally pull the trigger of his gun which may result in a fatality. But since the incident that brought me to the hospital, we had taken precaution through a 'buddy' treatment, calming each other in case the discussion got too spirited.

"Man must be neither meek as in the Christian ideal or strong as argued by Nietzsche. The better philosophy is that of living for others which John Stuart Mill[119] had advocated." A new twist in the conversation was interjected by Bebot, a student who was active in the union movement.

"These are socialist ideas. All men must contribute to everyone's interests. This is the theory of sympathetic affections, of pity, and of use to others," he added.

"It is a tempting idea. But remember in the end all these succumbed to man's ambition and his lust for power. Look at Lenin[120] and Stalin.[121] They were socialists but more aptly

---

[119] English philosopher and exponent of utilitarianism.

[120] Leader of the radical socialist party that became the Communist Party.

[121] Dictator of the USSR for 29 years.

called communists because of their emphasis on the absence of private ownership of property under the proletariat that holds supreme command. Karl Marx, [122] who was famous for this idea, did not advocate the killing of their own people. It is intolerance and totalitarian tendencies of the leaders that caused these murders. They are no different from authoritarian religious leaders who kill to preserve the supremacy of their faith, the basis of their power. Good ideas are poison in the hands of those with a fetish for control."

"Soulless." The term used by Santi to describe this kind of leader.

"The good and humane idea in the hands of one is worse than a whiskey bottle when he is drunk!" Bobby the Confucian [123] among us made a point while embracing his bottle of beer.

I admired the critical minds of my young colleagues who felt the country's dependence on the US must be broken if it expects to move forward and progress. We had yet to live and be tested in actual trenches of geopolitics.

Yet it was a good portent for the future.

---

[122] Though he was a German philosopher, he was best known as a revolutionary whose works inspired the foundation of many communist regimes.

[123] A person who believes in the teachings of the Chinese philosopher Confucius (respecting the elders, for one).

# 7

# BINONDO: A RUDE TASTE OF BUSINESS

I went to the port area the following Monday earlier than usual. At the gate to the company's compound, there was a crowd of employees waiting to enter the gate because of an unusual security check. I did not have the regular identification card for employees, so I just waited outside to be called.

The crowd was chattering in whispers, and it shocked me that the company yacht which was used to entertain business guests and VIPs had caught fire triggered by an explosion at dawn. There was an intense investigation going on, so a yellow line had been set up to prevent entry to the area where the dockside office was located. It was already lunchtime when the investigation was finally concluded.

While the damage was considerable, there were no injuries reported. The fire was alleged to be caused by faulty wiring but Mang[124] Enteng, the Head of Engineering thought otherwise. He had a personal interest in keeping the yacht safe and in tiptop condition. It was the only way his bosses directly engage him whenever they wanted to spend private hours cruising in Manila Bay, showing off to guests their executive perks. He knew that the faulty wiring theory is remote but

---

[124] Tagalog word for mister.

while it is untrue and unpleasant to admit it, the speculation about sabotage may deal more damage to the company's reputation.

The administrative investigation to hear my testimony was called off. It was found out that no company funds were used for any car tire purchases. There was a lingering rumour of political intrigue and character assassination which the Marcos operative[125] had talked to me about.

I came out of the incident unscathed. The dowdy boy still dazzled by the urban landscape, however, has acquired a new gait and mien that only confidence born of crisis can provide.

It was not only my perspective that widened. Now, my universe was expanding as well as my curiosity which my father had feared would lead me to the unknown where I was unprepared.

I knew my father realised that nothing would prepare me for a specific challenge except in a psychological way from stories of successes or failures or with the company of peers.

*

When the purchasers or buyers were paid their commission, they conveniently forgot to give me my allowance. I did not pester them for it, but I told myself that I can do their work as well. I heard them talk about Binondo[126] and a street called Gandara where cheap marine parts were sold.

Binondo was an ideal marketplace. Walking in the streets of Binondo was like walking side by side with the ghosts of

---

[125] A trusted staff for political activities.
[126] A district in Manila known as Chinatown.

four hundred years of global Chinese traders who changed the route of international trade to the Americas without passing through Europe. As early as 1600s, Binondo was already known all over the world as a place where silk, tapestries, kettles and cast-iron pots and gunpowder from China and many more were acquired and distributed for great profit all over the world. It was, therefore, an attractive destination for many Chinese who leave China in search of the proverbial goldmine. They brought with them their business practices and acumen, and the hardship of living away from home created those skills to survive and prosper. After hundreds of years in the Philippines, these immigrant Chinese own the banks, huge real estate property and displaced the American and British control of the country's economic blood flow.

Binondo was Chinatown which made Manila "the World's first global city" with 'Escolta', a street that was its Wall Street and the first business centre of the country. In a manner of speaking, it was the exclamation point of centuries of people-to-people interaction and trade between the Chinese and Filipinos. Pigafetta, [127] the diarist of Ferdinand Magellan, the first European to reach the Philippines, described the island King and Queen of Limasawa[128] "wearing Chinese silk and eating off Chinese porcelain; their houses had "silk curtains and porcelain ornaments", and "their trading currency was Chinese coins with square centres".

I told my plans to Richie Boy who told me he was thinking of the same thing. Our work ethic got a new boost that made

---

[127] An Italian scholar and explorer who went with Magellan in his voyage and one of the only 18 who got back to Spain afterwards.

[128] Island part of southern city of Cebu.

mining the piles of purchase orders for needed spare parts seem less tedious. We compiled invoices and made our own directory of stores and compared their prices. At the lunch break, we would go out of the port area to scout places indicated in the receipts. Because of the proximity of the school from Gandara, I got extra time to study.

It was business as usual to the regular purchasers. One afternoon, Mang Enteng, a retired merchant marine, called the purchasing office requesting urgently a new marine engine for one of the tugboats that were involved in a salvage operation in Manila. There was a deadline to produce the new engine otherwise the cost of demurrage to the company would be substantial. The regular purchasers were out after receiving their commission that day and Richie Boy and I were the only ones left of the staff.

Mang Enteng was a frail man, his body almost curved because of sclerosis, but he had this strong character needed in a hard environment like the port area. He knew his business and that any delay in the repair would adversely impact operations.

Responsibility for the burning of the yacht still weighed heavily on his shoulders and he did not want new trouble at his doorsteps. The troubles in the operation of tugboats were dropping like raindrops and the stoop that had developed in his walk betrayed his concern.

Richie Boy was quick to see an opening for us to do the purchasing ourselves. On his own, he approached the purchasing manager to allow us to purchase the engine in a Gandara store we had earlier identified. As fodder to his pitch, he apprised the purchasing manager that I had not been receiving the allowance promised by the regular purchasers. A man of unquestioned fairness, the boss was infuriated. He asked me to go to Binondo to make the purchase and he told me I could keep the commission.

If there was a disruption of the modus vivendi[129] in the purchasing routine, the assistant purchasing manager seemed to ignore it. He was contacting suppliers by phone, but he could not get through. The telephone system at that time was a mess yet he seemed to ignore the urgency. Talking with our feet would have been faster, but a few minutes later, I was on my way to Binondo.

When I went to the Gandara store, I told the sales clerk about our urgent need, but he refused to do business with me. He insisted on talking instead with the regular purchaser. I knew if I shopped around, there would be a store that would deal with me and perhaps even sell at a lower price. But there was no leeway for this because the grey marine engine was urgently needed. There was a deadline to deliver the engine and given my unfamiliarity with the area, I didn't have any time to shop around. There was a choice to be made between meeting the urgency of the replacement engine and the delay to afford the opportunity to break the collusion between the players in this theatre of business.

I chose time as value, but this meant finding the regular purchaser. I suspected I'd find him in one of the restaurants in Chinatown where they hang around after every transaction.

My hunch was right. Benjie, the regular purchaser, was there. He appeared half-smiling and half-growling, but his eyes betrayed which was his true emotion. He was terribly

---

[129] An arrangement or agreement allowing conflicting parties to co-exist peacefully.

peeved at me for encroaching upon his turf. He either ignored Richie Boy or he was playing safe with him because of his obvious connections. It gave me an insight into why some people are called sacred cows. I thought that in this battle for what is right, I will be the first casualty.

We told him we knew that he and the store salesman were in cahoots and that they had been overpricing everything. That was our ace. He grudgingly agreed to lower the price because of the possibility of being exposed and the ensuing embarrassment. I could tell he wasn't doing this because it was the right thing to do, but only cutting his losses. To us, it was a taste of triumph but to him, it was clear proof of our naivete. If he had decided to teach us a lesson or give us a dose of his scorn, it did not show.

The engine was delivered on time, payments were made, and Benjie got his fat commission. After that, he was absent for a few days and after spending all his easily earned commission, he came back for another transaction. Our boss has to squeeze from him our share of the commission and as he dipped into his pocket, he was breathing heavily trying to suppress a truculent look. It is not pride at all but the feeling of giving away what he thought he had earned. *This guy is worse than Mr Hot Head,* I thought.

Before he disappeared, he gave Richie Boy and me a piece of advice: "Your dedication is misplaced. After a day or two, you and Richie Boy could have had a bigger share." He sounded like there are more practical rules to be followed and that delay is 'de rigueur'[130] in a market like Binondo.

Why would a delay be an advantage? I asked myself. Such

---

[130] French meaning "out of strict etiquette".

curiosity only comes from inexperience. Benjie contributed to my thickening knowledge of the value of time. In this case, Benjie and his colleagues used the urgency with which we needed the engine to unscrupulously monetise time.

*

The fruits of our labour encouraged me to count imaginary profits and build castles in my mind. Binondo is the seat of an ideal market and even the likes of Benjie can succeed. The rules seemed simple. We had the added advantage of having the purchase orders at our fingertips. The suppliers are in place; we can negotiate for the best price and make the best bargains. My head was spinning like a calculator.

My new business pursuit reminded me of my mother's going to Bangar, La Union to buy *'abel'* to sell for a small profit in Isabela. Her business model was straightforward. In Binondo, there were unwritten rules which gave them substantial earnings yet most of those rules are unethical. The mantra of honour among thieves strengthens and holds together collusions and alliances of people to land a deal and make tremendous profits. Our feet were stepping up to the door of the living world of free enterprise, different from the theoretical discourses in the canteen, forewarned by that open war with those already entrenched like Benjie and company.

The prospect of doing my own commerce gave me high hopes but unrealistic expectations. With financial security came greater independence, I thought. I figured out that I was still young. Perhaps, I would reduce my load of subjects or skip a semester to devote myself to business.

In the short period that I was in Manila, my ethos was

shaping up in many directions. I became a libertarian like many of my friends at the canteen which demands a certain level of ethical responsibility to complement our newfound freedom. I felt it was important to remain true to the canteen's collective idea of good even when conducting business in a place as rough as Binondo.

\*

When I was at the canteen, my friends were surprised when I volunteered to buy a round of drinks. This time my good friend, Manny, was with us at the table and they remembered him from the hospital where he'd introduced himself as my brother. They knew he was not really my brother, but that we had a close relationship like a brotherly bond.

"What is the occasion?" Santi asked. I know my friends were curious about what happened in my case at the office.

"There was an explosion; the case was closed, and I am going into business," I told them, catching my breath with excitement.

"Your case and the fire are related," Manny said.

It was part of the plot to destroy Marcos. It seems that politics and business are strange bedfellows.

Before Manny could say anything, I steered the conversation away from politics.

Having fallen to the charms of Binondo, I was at a crossroads.

"I will quit school for a semester, earn first and save for law school."

Going to law school was the preoccupation of this young group, not politics.

There was silence and disappointment on their faces.

"We are all working students and despite this handicap, we have high marks in all our subjects. We will all graduate together and go to law school, graduate and serve the people."

It summed up why we were there: not to prepare ourselves for the kind of business I was presently enthused by but the business of service to the people. It was another lofty idea.

Harry, the student from mountain province, injected an emotional and patriotic drift but he said it in a facetious way. It helps him that he is on scholarship because he belongs to the ethnic community in the mountain provinces and his father is a tribal leader.

A Visayan student whose parents were sugar plantation workers agreed with me.

"Go for financial security first. I can give you a hand," he volunteered.

This was the first time Conrad the Visayan joined the discussion. I liked Conrad's manner and his kind and soft speech as an Ilonggo. The contrasting opinion between the student from the north and the one from the south of Manila, the capital city, mirrored the different cultures and priorities of the Filipinos at that time.

Santi advised me to think it over. He knew my escape from the province and the sacrifices I had made to continue my college education in Manila.

"I have a good opportunity to earn." I explained the business model.

"It is not easy, and it is not safe," Manny said. "Those people live through their commissions, and you will be a threat to their business. For all you know the purchasing manager or someone in the purchasing department is part of the group.

That department is rotten like most of the purchasing departments in any company. Now that you know about the overpricing, you are a marked man."

"One swallow does not make a summer!" Another student, Joel, interjected in reference to the commission I received which encouraged me to change plans and priorities.

"The road to hell is paved with good intentions!" was the bold aside of JQ. There were talks of being forewarned and forearmed.

These one-liners had enriched our dialogue in the canteen and the eagerness to show off was tolerated and the lack of censure and mockery made our talks a lively time and much anticipated. It has become a game of giving aphorisms impromptu around the table while drinking beer. We had always carried with us a pocketbook of quotations which we had kept with us long after those years as a legacy of that peripatetic kind of a school.

Manny's statement, however, sounded a warning bell that made us feel that real life in business or in any profession is not a catwalk but full of dangerous traps. Admittedly, Manny has matured beyond his age and is street-smart. I have yet to know him better.

I was disturbed by Manny's statement. It made me think back and flashed in my mind the many times that Benjie and the assistant purchasing manager were always in a huddle in a corner of the office.

"Can you follow the rule of silence there? The port area is no man's land." Manny was clearly our mentor where real and practical work is involved. He was a good addition to our group, and he represented reality. We were all about philosophies and abstract thoughts with feet suspended in the air.

"This will happen to those who are holier-than-thou!" Santi made a sign language like slashing his throat with a knife. He may have been reading a lot of Mafia novels.

It is all coming back to me. Did Mang Enteng really need the engine desperately that day? Is the assistant purchasing manager the real big boss? Is he really calling the shots in the deals? Had Benjie deliberately disappeared to add pressure to the price going up? How many times has this business plot been repeated in Binondo for all these centuries past, and how many lives lost and wasted in its wake?

"In Binondo, there is a business culture which was hundreds of years in the making. We will already be finished in our studies, but you may just have scratched the surface of its depth. In that challenge to understand, perhaps learning from books and from those who have been in the trenches may just be faster and broader than informal learning in a lifetime." This was Santi's final advice.

\*

Now Socrates' advice of an unexamined life meets reality. Appearances are not what they are, after all, or they are only the tip of bigger things. Knowledge of the facts is important but how to deal with them is wisdom. I began to learn the fundamentals of being street-smart and recognising that to live is an art by itself. The attitude of scepticism developed at this stage in my life served me well as a lawyer later.

A mistake or slight miscalculation when judging people and events at face value would be fatal. Each incident presents new circumstances to be seen from a new perspective. It could be according to one's expectations like material gain or fame, or power, or even gaining new friends or associates, or simply for peace of mind. There is no standard approach, except to know the facts first and decide based on experience and common sense. Whether to act or not to act requires courage and patience.

The sharing of knowledge deduced from borrowed ideas with my colleagues at the canteen illuminated the realities I had heard like a thunderbolt, seen as lightning and felt like rain while at work in the port area. There was a process of cross-pollination between ideas at the canteen and experiences at the workplace which shaped my approach to life. My frustrations and unfulfilled expectations had so far given me a life that was rich, unique and worth telling.

I recalled Benjie's face which now becomes a picture of death, violence, and intimidation while on the flipside, the lure of big income. This is how the talk drifted as my colleagues pondered on my life's trajectory. The mental thread consists of enjoying material things that lead to profanity but spiritual deprivation. The zest of the previous hours fuelled by optimism which was part reverie and part erstwhile experience is lost. They saw me staring blankly at the wall and correctly guessed that I was feeling desolate.

I did not blame my friends for the final effect on me of the exchanges. They led me to realise that there are more responsibilities and challenges created with my newfound life of freedom living alone in Manila.

There was another reason that gave me sleepless nights. I and my Chinese friend back in the province, the huckster and my business collaborator, were reunited in Binondo where he was employed with his uncle in one of the Gandara marine parts stores. He heard about the incident and warned me to stay clear of Binondo as it was not safe for me.

All of this made me feel guilty for abandoning the person who had been my most reliable guide to life. It has given me a sense of loss and regret. The concerns in my young life defined my freedom but looking back I now realise this was a farce.

As I missed my father, I yearned for the security and peace of home.

I remembered the shell shown to me by Tata Abon and the feeling of peace and hope brought about by the hissing sound of time. When I told my father about Tata Abon's shell, he laughed aloud as I have never seen him laugh. Then he said Tata Abon is rich with memories and the shell must remind him of younger years filled with hope for the future.

He sounded as though he was not only talking about Tata Abon but also about his own beautiful and memorable past.

It is a beautiful tale I have to share later!

\*

# 8
# THE LANGUAGE OF THE SOUL

Meanwhile…

Music was a common interest among the students in the canteen. When the jukebox played, everybody listened and this gave us a respite from our usual verbal scrimmages, a time to be pensive, to take stock of our circumstances. The songs of Paul Anka, Neil Sedaka, Anita Bryant, Nat King Cole, Johnny Mathis, Matt Monro were among the favourites. The Filipino version of these greats then were Pilita Corrales, Eddie Mesa, Bobby Gonzales, and The Reycard Duet. The last duo had made a name for themselves performing in Las Vegas. Carding, the other half of the Reycard Duet, was rumoured later to be a close friend of Lana Turner, famous American actress, a cause to make Filipino 'machismo' celebrate vicariously. It was three years before Gemma Cruz, a great grandniece of Jose Rizal, the Filipino national hero, was crowned Miss International and Gloria Diaz as Miss Universe.

One evening someone played Elvis Presley's gospel song, 'Mansion over the Hilltop'.

I thought I saw my father in the corner of my eye. When I followed the figure, he immediately disappeared. I asked a student who played the gospel song about the man he was talking with earlier. He is one of the older students who were already graduating, he assured me. I had not taken my meal the whole day, so I blamed it on hunger hallucination. Like a good Samaritan, he instructed the cashier to take care of my order with his change since he was leaving and could not wait for her to come back. He left before I could resist.

"I was there that night when the music was being played but I did not show my presence. Looking at my son behind the curtain I saw a young man very different from the boy I know and thought that he was reborn in many ways. I understood and resisted the urge to embrace him."

My wife revealed what my father told her many years later. It was not mere imagination when I saw his likeness in a corner outside the canteen.

"When your husband was born, I was in church waiting for my time to render my sermon. There is this beautiful gospel music sang by the choir of the church when another good piece of music was whispered to me. It was news that my wife delivered a baby boy. I thought then that he embodies all the work that I have done and for him to be born while I was doing God's ministry, I would call him God's work." My wife recalled my father's words.

That was in the distant past and I cannot imagine how to react then. I would have broken down, the new life force breaking into pieces, the new strength would have given way to a nostalgic feeling to return to a father I had misunderstood, or I could have fought against my true feelings and put more distance between him and me. To a dutiful son, the first would have been instinct but to one who has mounted a high horse may just refuse and gallop his way to his pride and fall.

"Your father was pulled by two hard choices, to embrace you back but he knew that would weaken you or leave you in the ring being pummelled by the hard punches of life and it was painful for him to decide to let you go that night!" My wife commented appearing to be neutrally perceptive, but I knew my father had confided his thoughts to her.

Seeing the inquisitiveness in my wife's eyes, I continued to tell her what happened that night in the canteen so she could understand the moral choices I made since my escape.

Elvis kept singing:

*'I'm satisfied with just a cottage below*
*a little silver and a little gold*
*but in that city where the ransomed shine*
*I want a gold one that has silver line*
*I 've got a mansion just over the hilltop*
*in that bright land where we 'll never grow old*
*and someday yonder we will never more wonder*
*but walk on streets that are the purest gold.'*

The song a 'Mansion Over the Hilltop' was in the centre of my father's work and mission. The lyrics made me remember him; a thought which is a burden and also an impetus. It was played every time by the same student to the point that I felt irritated because feeling guilty is hard to avoid.

*Who is this student? Why is he fond of this song? Is there a conspiracy to haunt me?* These thoughts always intrigued me. At the same time, I longed for my father to appear at the canteen where we would reunite. Then I would be back to the old proven path a son should take but then I realised it would mean losing the chance of a lifetime. Too many conflicting thoughts that tore me apart.

My musings stopped when someone commented:

"I like this music. I feel like God is with me," Hermie, one of the students, was moved by the song. He is a transferee like me but he came from a seminary in Manila and not from the province.

I looked around. All of them were silent but their eyes were staring blankly as their thoughts were seeing their inner core instead, trying to find some meaning within. There is some eloquence with their aggregate silence.

"When I attend the Catholic mass, I feel the lack of candour among people in performing the religious rituals," he added.

"Even in non-Catholic masses, there is a lot of artificiality. Their voices are contrived to make an emotional effect. Hypocrisy is abundant in all these religious activities, Catholic, Protestant or any other denomination," Rody weighed in.

He added:

"But when you hear a piece of music like that where there are no labels of faith, no sectarian affinity at all but pure thought of a power bigger than anything, there is a lot of spirituality," he added.

Why is there hypocrisy when religion is formalised? Why is there a feeling of so much peace when the language of the soul is pure music?

It is because in organised worship the idea of worship becomes a transaction between man and the church, which is different from a one-way communication to the sublime when a man just reflects or meditates for grace and mercy!

Someone may have read me or that the thought dawned on all of us. But we did not dare say more for fear that we may lose its purity. There is a clarity per se in it to even pause to reason.

While Elvis kept on singing, I could feel everyone longing

to fill a void or experiencing a thirst that no water could quench, or hunger that no food could satiate. I remembered my father saying that 'man does not live by bread alone', quoting the scriptures. That I believe.

"God is what you feel in your heart. It is a faith that there is a Supreme Being. God has no form and no image at all. You cannot call God 'him' or 'her'; God has no gender." Harry, the scholar from Mountain Province was the first to give in.

We allowed Harry, the scholar, and Hermie, the seminarian, to do the exchanges. There is a great wealth of knowledge about theology between them. No one bothered to remind them of the rules against discussing religion.

We were mesmerised by the originality of their thoughts.

"God is not a person who consciously rewards or punishes. Divine punishment or reward are consequences of breaking or upholding the principles of order, unity, growth, decline, and death inherent in creation. We are a tiny part of the creation which is subject to the logic of time according to Ecclesiastes," Hermie emphasised.

"You may think that you have evaded punishment when you commit a crime or violation without anybody knowing your crime. Or you think you are too strong and powerful. But time does not stand still. Time goes on until your crime is revealed. Then you are punished or maybe events had already occurred to equalise like a weighing scale," Hermie continued.

"It is like planting a fruit tree. With sunlight, water, and soil combined, in time the tree bears its fruits. Then you get your reward. That natural consequence is God's way to intervene," Harry said in agreement. As a native of the mountain provinces, he has a close affinity with nature. Animism was still practiced and believed in the more remote areas of his province.

I thought of the sleepless nights, missed meals, the time spent in the canteen imbibing knowledge and wisdom from the erudition of my classmates and colleagues not just passing events. Under God's time, there will be the certainty of reward and that is the truth about him.

One of the students, Susing, came forward with a Bible. He read the seven days of creation which he claims to be in conflict with science.

"The Bible is written mostly in allegory to excite the popular mind. The people could not have believed in creation if it were reckoned in millions of years of evolution. There was no Garden of Eden and there is no Adam and Eve. The dialogue between God and a man in Genesis were metaphors or a literary license to explain, among others, the concept of right and wrong!" Teddy remarked.

"Now that science — and particularly with the means of archaeology — had proved that the world was a billion years in the making, which to God may just be a timeless second, only the message of right and wrong remains true," he added.

Like a thunderbolt, I realised then and there that God is a pure thought coming from a spring of truth within oneself, independent of and untouched by the dogma and the imagery of an organised religion or sect. The story of speaking to God would be inconsistent with this concept.

This canteen and the many exchanges had been our island of Tarsus[131] where Paul the apostle found his epiphany.

"How do Jesus Christ, the prophets, Mohammad, Buddha and the other great founders of religious movements figure in

---

[131] An ancient city in Turkey.

this concept of God?" Celso asked with the seriousness of one who is genuinely interested to know.

Hermie replied:

"They all preached the golden rule. All actions must be in fulfilment of love, charity, fairness."

"How about the afterlife? There is the resurrection of Jesus as clear proof?" Celso asked.

The number of the circle around Hermie had thickened.

The belief in Jesus was shared by everyone there and the story of his resurrection was the climax that ensured the success of the religious movement in his name.

There was a long silence. Every eye was on Hermie. I thought that if Jesus' resurrection is disproved then the Christian religion will lose its foundation. Then pandemonium will break loose among the believers.

"I believe that Jesus' message of love, charity, and fairness are the ingredients of a personal and community order and peace on earth. This is what counts and, in the process, will get you a reward in this world. I am referring to a historical Jesus who may have lived more than a thousand years ago. There was a Jesus whose nature was the subject of controversy whether he was a God or Man in the Council of Nicaea five hundred years after the death of Jesus of Nazareth. Nonetheless, I do hope that there is an afterlife to reward those good people with good hearts. What is the good of believing in the resurrection when the bad is unpunished?"

Hermie is hard to crack.

"We want to know if there is an afterlife?" Celso asked.

"Galileo once said that the 'earth is not the centre of the universe'. He was forced to retract otherwise they would have killed him. Now, everyone believes that the earth circles around the sun. Galileo's ideas and the Garden of Eden had been proven as mere allegory by science and modern discoveries are changing our beliefs." Jack, another student, intervened before Hermie could talk.

"No one has experienced another Lazarus though men of science may try to undergo a clinical death momentarily to experience what happens after the flatline. Our limited life may not have a chance to know the truth on the afterlife," Hermie speculated.

This time Hermie was deliberately off-tangent. But I know Hermie. His remark was just bait. He must be leading on to something and I was anxious to find out what it was.

I looked around and imagined who would take the bait and I was not disappointed. It was Rody.

"A Jesuit priest fondled my private part in the confessional in the grade school," he said in his straightforward manner. Everyone laughed except him.

We could not believe it. But Rody was serious, and he was fuming mad. "I hope there is an afterlife where one could either go to heaven or to hell," he said. "That Jesuit priest will burn in hell, I am sure."

There is always a reason why ideas or beliefs come into man's thought!

"Maybe not, maybe he will go to purgatory. But he might be transferred to heaven after many prayers of devotion and contributions to the church. This is what we hear from the men of God," Celso suggested smiling.

There was a chorus of laughing and jeering at the same time at the thought of purgatory, long peddled by the church, and to escape from it required the faithful to pay. These payments funded the building of cathedrals and built armies of mercenaries in the Middle Ages.

The heightened emotion generated by Rody's revelation was greater than the sum of our individual interest in the afterlife. The loosening of the grip of the Catholic faith in many of us was hard to ignore.

"When we close our eyes and think of God, any image conceived is wrong for no one has seen God. The authors of the Bible believed in God but cannot conceive God of what He is like. The closest to it is a metaphor of a ball of fire and voice for the purpose of conveying the reality of a Supreme Being."

A man of mature age whom I noticed to have been listening and observing calmed us down.

"You are fortunate that you are no longer living at the time when the church was in power. All of you would have been guillotined before sunrise tomorrow."

He continued, "Thinking of God in the image of man is the first big mistake. How can one created make a conscious image of its creator?

"All of religion made God a piece of merchandise. The story of the gospel is part of their sales tools. Religion is a business enterprise. It was so successful that they gained wealth and power. And they killed, wholesale massacre, because of this!" he went on.

I asked one of my friends who the guy was and he said he is a retired professor of philosophy at our university. He was a campus celebrity during his time. They liked and respected him.

Santi took it from there: "No church is needed; no cathedrals to be built; no business ritual masquerading as religion to be undertaken.

"We need to believe in a Supreme Being," he pointed out.

"It is this belief that fills up a man's existential need. He may have realised this as early as his hunting days. He saw manifestation in the skies, lightning here and thunderstorm there; the wind that blew over the leaves and trunks of trees; the echoes of animals carousing or in intercourse… all of these are mystic sounds which he took as the mystic sounds of someone far greater or more powerful. He respected all these phenomena which his senses felt, heard, or saw. Then he began to pray to them for a favour, for protection, for healing; for the bounty from the land and from the water. Then, he had a concept of the gods."

He was talking about the evolution of belief in God.

He made a fearless forecast. "The whole religious institution as we know now will collapse. We will carry our faith in our hearts. That will be the way people will worship God in the future."

Santi's statement was met with general cynicism this time. Silence usually followed after he explained confidently his theories and beliefs. Hermie remarked that despite his break from the Catholic Church he thinks that there is no way it will lose its power and influence. Even the other religious sects and denominations will all grow in numbers. People need to cling to something or be strengthened by psychological support systems which these organisations can provide in times of economic and family crises. Besides, these churches and their schools have become powerful in business and politics and can reduce a man who does not share their beliefs to a pariah in social interactions.

"As we ponder all these things in our humble corner of this world, educational institutions run by the religious will produce a formidable army of defenders in the false god, the trinity and the religious prescription for rituals. We have no match for them," Hermie continued.

Hermie was a pragmatist!

Then, in support of the professor, another cited the tragic end to the Albigensian crusade[132] in the 12th and 13th centuries.

"The Albigensian, in 12th and 13th century in southern France, were an anti-sacerdotal movement in opposition to the Roman church clergy whom they claimed to be corrupt. They were labeled as heretics. During the papacy of Innocent III, the Catholics resorted in mass killings of the Albigensian whom they considered as heretics. There were complaints from the Catholic crusaders themselves that the killings were indiscriminate, even the non-heretics, dismissing these concerns that by a caveat that 'God' tell them apart. These are different times but there are ways by which they will deprive you of an opportunity to do business or gain employment by reason of your belief. This will be as bad as death."

Everyone in my cluster of friends contributed stories from their readings about religious intolerance. One tragic story is the massacre of five to ten thousand French Protestants by French Catholics in less than twenty-four hours on 23 August 1572. The Pope in Rome, happy with the bloodletting of the church's opposition, dedicated a fresco to the massacre in one of the Vatican rooms. Since then, that day was called 'St Bartholomew's Day'.

Now, there are Muslim fundamentalists who kill under the guise of doing it for Allah but in truth, it is for the exercise of power and greed.

---

[132] Christian movement in southern France asserting the coexistence of two mutually opposed principles: one good and one evil.

Santi summed it up: "In the recorded history of three hundred years from the crucifixion of Jesus to Constantine's conversion, Christians slaughtered Christians in the millions for slight deviations in the interpretation of Jesus' gospel of understanding, tolerance, love and compassion."

There was a long silence. We were all confounded by how faith in God is so simple but became too complicated because man wants to be exclusive with his claim about true worship. He uses power and intolerance to preserve that exclusive claim.

Something is wrong somewhere.

"Let us all go to church this Sunday."

We laughed at the spontaneity of the remark. That's it. When we filed out of the canteen, almost everybody must have realised how hard it is to kick old habits.

*

Then it was late 1971.

The exegesis on religion was brought about by a song entitled 'Imagine' by John Lennon. The song despised government, religion and possessions. His popularity, however, did not diminish. The song came when the streets of Manila were on fire and filled with students demonstrating. People's distrust in government had grown to its highest levels.

Many of my friends were bewildered that I liked Elvis Presley's 'Mansion over the Hilltop' and John Lennon's 'Imagine' at the same time. To them, the songs conveyed opposing messages. All of us clung to the faith and hope in God which the spirit of Elvis' song conveyed. It is the legacy of our long night at the canteen.

"Lennon was referring to the bad side of religion," I argued. There are rituals which are not necessary. It is merely an instrument to generate wealth and power. They remembered these thoughts. It was déjá vu.[133]

The faithful are yet to know that they are being victimised. They are clinging to the merchants of hope.

There is nothing in Lennon's message that negates belief in God. He speaks of a dream and to dream means to have faith and hope in a Supreme Being. This is a relationship to a Supreme Being that is personal and not through the agency of an organised religion. There is no toll or license fee to have faith in God or even salvation. To label Lennon as anti-God is misplaced. He rejects the *religion* which is in the class of greed and evil power.

I conjured a musical conversation between Elvis and Lennon. The message of Lennon is that Presley must not care about the gold and silver lining but just walk with God in pure peace to have his mansion. John Lennon dreams that peace is possible in this real world. They both longed for spirituality. Had they met and reflected on their songs, they might not have died early; alas, one from the bullet of an assassin, the other very high on the bathroom floor.

They appeared bored by the topic, and they only came alive when I mentioned Lennon's assassination and Elvis's death from an overdose. I thought that their priority had changed after seven years since we last met at the canteen and now, they are less enthusiastic about religion. I complained to a colleague who was one of the canteen's habitués about this

---

[133] French meaning 'already seen'.

transformation. He is now a respected judge.

He said, "Didn't you notice that while we grew older, the force that fuelled our interest went down below the waist? As we grow older it will shift back to the mind. That is when you must write your story before you start to forget, then senility and final rest."

And then as lawyers, he added seriously, they may have seen loopholes in the anti-religion arguments then promoted by our celebrity professor. Or that they don't care as long as a man who had been a bad boy when young became a better person at a later age because a faith in God has transformed him. In that sense, religion is no longer about the afterlife; the more important thing being that faith in a Supreme Being could change a person or a society for the better.

*

When religion is stripped of commercialism it relieves itself from complexity and its simplicity tunes in man directly to a genuine belief in a Supreme Being whose presence and meaning in his life nourishes his spirit. The concept of God then becomes a concept of goodness.

This is precisely what President Thomas Jefferson[134] of the United States did. He read through the gospel and cut out a lot of miracles and those passages he could not understand. There was no reference to any virgin birth and the end was the rolling of the stone against the tomb of Jesus. For him, the true Bible must be read as a benevolent code of morals of pure principles which came from the very words of Jesus. He

---

[134] 3rd President of the US (1801 – 1809).

removed the artificial vestments which the priests 'muffled' and "travestied into various forms, as instruments of riches and power to themselves". He called his book *The Life And Morals of Jesus of Nazareth.*[135]

I recalled a story in *The Brothers Karamazov*[136] about a saint who took mercy of a beggar who was hungry and frozen. The saint "took him into his bed, held him in his arms, and began breathing into his mouth, which was putrid and loathsome from some awful disease". He did it as an act of duty to his faith. Perhaps, I thought, that this random act of kindness, or even madness if one looks at it that way, if done out of pure and simple love, would mean that one would be closer to God's grace than if it were an act of faith to earn the afterlife.

My distance from my father widened even more after the discourse!

---

[135] Better known as the Jefferson Bible, his own compilation of the four gospels in The New Testament. He bent over the book, using razor and scissors cutting out the small squares of texts.

[136] Russian novel by Dostoevsky.

# 9
# ISLAM: A FAITH THAT CARES

Sunday mornings, I have to be in Luneta, or what is now known as Rizal Park, for my ROTC[137] or student military training.

My feelings about Luneta had always been ambivalent. ROTC training forced me to wake up at five o'clock in the morning and don the military khaki uniform for four hours of training under the hot sun.

My experience with my company commander who was a Muslim introduced me to Islam.

The training in the model company was harsh. Our cadet officer was very strict, and the drills were precise. It was exacting. His template was the Philippine Military Academy in Baguio City, an elite military school attracting even foreign students from nearby Asian countries.

It was in my fourth semester of ROTC training that the company cadet commander became an acquaintance. He was a classmate in one of the evening classes and he remembered me to be in his company.

"Why are you late taking up the ROTC?" he asked me.

"I am a transferee. There was no ROTC training in the three semesters that I was in the province."

---

[137] Reserve Officer Training Corps.

It was really peculiar because when I started my first semester of ROTC, my batchmates in our year level were already on the fourth and last semester of training.

"You are thin and underweight," he said.

I said I was a working student.

"Next Sunday" he said, "you don't have to be in formation. Your assignment is to prepare the refreshments during breaks."

The following Sunday, and the other Sundays after that, I was in the shade preparing our company's soft drinks and sandwiches. That started our long friendship. I learnt later that compassion is one of the bedrocks of the Muslim faith.

He was from Mindanao. He wanted to be the first in his town to be a military officer, but he was not admitted at the Philippine Military Academy.

He was tall and heavyset. The way he spoke betrayed his rural origin. Even if he was not in uniform, he would be wearing his military cadet shoes. Because of the sound the shoes made, you always knew when he was approaching the classroom even if you were concentrating on your notes.

We wrote a term paper together along with another classmate. It was about bringing the Muslims and Christians together in one cohesive community. Even then it was about ownership of lands and the lack of economic opportunity of many of the Muslims. He admitted that many Muslims are entrepreneurial especially the Maranaos [138] and that the Tausugs [139] were more education orientated. Like in the Christian community, there were rich Muslims and poor

---

[138] Southern indigenous people who lived mostly on the lake in stilts.

[139] One of the largest of the southern Muslim ethnic group.

Muslims. The foot soldiers of the Muslim secessionist movement come from the poor but the rich and educated Muslims take sides where the winning tide goes. It boils down to who gets power and the weaker are fodder to these ambitions. It was a crash course on the evolution of the Muslim secession.

After graduation, he joined the Philippine Army and when I met him again, he was already a colonel.

*

His kindness made me curious about the Muslim faith. I warmed up to the practical idea of a man allowed to marry at least four wives. But there is a compelling ethical, moral and economic reason for this. One is taking an orphan to be a wife as a means of support, another is taking a widow as a wife so she will not be living in a scandal. There must be a compelling justifying circumstance.

In a religion that enforces monogamy like Catholicism, there are many who have more wives than Muslims. Most if not all of those Muslim men I know, only have one wife.

Not this one. Many years later, there was a friend who was of high social standing. I visited him for some business. His phone rang and he said that it was "L", his second wife, a senator. He asked the secretary to call another woman, his first wife. He told me that his first wife is in the penthouse and the second wife is on another floor. To answer my quizzical look, he showed me a certification that he was a convert to the Muslim faith.

*

Ever since I arrived in Manila, my curiosity was limitless. This included venturing into an examination of other religious faiths.

What made them tick? Why should there be Muslims, Christians, Jews, Buddhists? It is this diversity, I thought, that makes life interesting. Without it, it is boring. The natural landscape is beautiful because of its varied colours. There is no fighting in nature in the gradual process of change.

On the other hand, differences in religion cause gore, disquiet and mass displacements. The belief systems which start as naturally simple evolve into colourful rituals. Genuineness is replaced by artificiality. Pure devotion in the heart becomes idolization. The matter of the soul becomes an earthly business with all the attendant intrigue, cunning, and profiteering of the marketplace. Alas, this human fall has been consistent in all religions and follows a pattern from the initial stages of their evolution. While their early adherents underwent prosecution, fuel to the trajectory of their growth, in time their growth and success turn them into persecutors themselves. They became lions and tigers, the predators in their environment.

In this light, Jesus correctly said that only the meek and the lamb will be welcome in his home as the template of acceptable religious reverence. This may be why many of the men of the cloth, priests or pastors, speak softly and saintly to camouflage wittingly or unwittingly what religions had become. But then the Bible warned of men in 'sheep's clothing' but a wolf inside, nevertheless.

I saw the Muslim faith as practical in the way it practises universal love and compassion. What becomes ugly are those who adhere to it for their own personal gain. Like my friend who converted out of convenience or those fanatics who wrongly use the faith for power and domination. When both Jesus and the prophet Muhammed return, they will surely be merciless on these people.

*

Word had gone around that I have left for the city to study. They know that I have been missing church services, that I have been associated with students who are free thinkers, and that I have been close to a Muslim ROTC officer. It dawned to me that the church's chain of command had been busy monitoring my movements. The church police were hard at work and their reports set alarm bells ringing in the church's hierarchy. Not that I am important, but my father occupied a high ministerial position, and I would be a precedent that may open floodgates of similar church youth to re-examine their faith. They are racing against time as I was gaining confidence in having independent thought.

The church had a great stake here. I will be an embarrassment to the church, and I am a potential eye-opener to other members. My father will suffer the consequences. He could be relieved of his duties in the ministry and that would kill him. He had sacrificed a lot to help build the church and he did not want his work to go down the drain. It is his passport to the mansion at the hilltop.

I was facing expulsion and then, ostracism.

One day my situation was the focus of discussion by my student friends at the canteen. The stories I heard were revealing.

Santi asked me: "Have you heard of Spinoza?" [140]

"He was a Jew and a philosopher," I said about the little I knew of him.

"He was excommunicated from the Jewish faith because of heresy," Santi continued. Excommunication is the extinction of a person's religious affiliation. To the Jews, it is to be outcast from the people of their race.

"It was not only his doubts on Judaism that compelled the Jewish community of Amsterdam to excommunicate him. It was more for political reasons," added another student whose name I cannot now remember.

"Yes, he struck against both the Jewish and Christian doctrine. The Jews there escaped from the Catholic inquisition in Spain and Portugal. It was the Christian Amsterdam that gave them refuge and tolerated their religious practice. They were grateful to Amsterdam and were embarrassed by Spinoza's heretical questioning of the Christian faith," Santi clarified.

"In the Jewish law during that time, to be excommunicated means to be cut off from his community unless the offender retracts which was very humiliating. A young Jewish man even shot himself in embarrassment after undergoing the formula of retraction." Santi was referring to Uriel Acosta [141] who wrote against the core Christian belief about the existence of an afterlife.

Later Spinoza wrote about his ex-communication:

*"...those who wish to seek out the causes of miracles, and*

---

[140] Dutch philosopher known for his ethics.

[141] Portuguese philosopher who was born Christian but converted to Judaism and ended up questioning the Catholic and rabbinic institutions of his time.

*to understand the things of nature as philosophers, and not to stare at them in astonishment like fools, are soon considered heretical and impious, and proclaimed as such by those whom the mob adore as the interpreters of nature and the gods. For these men that once ignorance is put aside that wonderment would be taken away which is the only means by which their authority is preserved."*

I had started to question the claim of my church that there is no salvation outside it. All Protestants, Catholics, Jews, Muslims, and those of other religions will all go to hell because they are not members of the church. How about these friends of mine whom I know as good people, will they also burn in hell?

I was in a quandary.

There were men of crime and bad habits who have become good and useful because they believe in the church. They were desperate and hopeless, yet they found a new life after their conversion. Definitely, the church, like any other, serves also a specific transforming value. If it were to benefit society, I thought, the claim about exclusive salvation through the "last messenger of God" can just be left to pass. That this is a lie does not make the church irrelevant.

But some danger lurks with the church police who could be turned into a passionate mob as Spinoza had observed. They could be the toy and tool of religious leaders who veer away from the mission of love to their greed for power, wealth and fame. These things corrupt the soul.

In these modern times, however, the use of force, violence, and intimidation may no longer be as flagrant. But the church is no less dangerous. For one born to this church, its punishment will be more of ostracism and the loss of the natural and social support systems.

Spinoza underwent the humiliating process of excommunication but was able to deal with the extreme ostracism of his race because the Christians of Amsterdam embraced him as one of them. He never converted though. When he died, somebody quipped that the last of the Christians had died.

I learnt from my friends how great men dealt with religion in different ways.

For Sigmund Freud, [142] "when a man is freed of religion, he has a better chance to live a normal and wholesome life."

Mohandas K. Gandhi[143] was more universal: "I consider myself a Hindu, Christian, Moslem, Jew, Buddhist, and Confucian."

While my friends debated religion, I closed my eyes and pondered about my father. My relationship with him was at the centre of any decision to break or not from this church.

---

[142] Austrian neurologist and the founder of psychoanalysis.

[143] Indian lawyer and anti-colonial nationalist who led the movement against the British rule of India.

PART TWO

# 10
# REMEMBERING A FATHER'S LEGACY

"Goose pimples rose all over me, my hair stood on end, my eyes filled with tears of love and gratitude for this greatest of all conquerors of human misery and shame, and my breath came in little gasps."

These words described someone's excessive zeal for a cause, the very feeling that raised an arm in salute to the ancient Roman Legions, or the emotion behind the gesture by the fanatics of Hitler in modern times. I saw it in my father for his church and I never doubted his sincerity nor questioned the logic behind it. In my case, I have already lost that feeling for the church with my enlightenment at the canteen but the emotion that bound me to my father remained strong.

Now, the time has come for that lost feeling to be rekindled. The church, where my father was one of the top ministers, will hold the fiftieth anniversary of its founding in 1964.

It was unfortunate, however, that a year before, the church suffered great distress with the death of its founder, Felix Manalo, after a lingering illness. He was calm in meeting his creator with the thought that he was leaving it in the hands of a very capable successor who was by his side during the hard days of the church and whom he prepared to take over. The death further heightened the religious fervour of the church faithful.

At this period, my distance was gradually widening from the church on many fronts, particularly on doctrinal issues. However, I have to admit that Felix Manalo was a beloved in my childhood and my scepticism about his doctrine of exclusive salvation never changed my estimate of him as a great soul. The same is true with his son and successor, Eraño Manalo, whom I considered an administrator par excellence. When the latter died, many were sceptical about whether he approved of his son Eduardo to take over as there were talks that Eraño or Ka Erdy preferred his son Felix, who was also called Angel because he was named after his grandfather. There were even talks that he had excommunicated Eduardo before his death which rumour did not gain traction. But it was not lost on the senior ministers of the church that the founder himself had anointed Eduardo to take over after his father and this prevailed.

My affiliation with the church hung on my father's personal story that holds me like a thread with a tensile strength.

\*

Tata Abon was one of the principal sources of the story of my father.

He talked of my father's loss of his only sister who was his spiritual guide and pilot of his youthful exuberance. Her absence has created a void to be filled up with something more meaningful and real. At this time, my father was still dizzily coping with the annihilation of the radical peasant group he had earlier joined.

The story of my father's ministry began at a propitious time when he was weak in spirit yet yearning for meaning and direction in his life.

An evangelical group sought refuge in his home. When the leader of that group asked him to join them in their sorties, candidly telling him to leave his home, he was an easy prey and he consented. Initially, it may have been an attractive novelty to a restless rebel or a sympathetic feeling for a well-meaning but ragtag group whose aim was to evangelise people to a new way of Christian practice and belief.

My father did not plan for a longer commitment. He did not foresee being with them permanently, but miracles happened and his decision, tentatively at first, became a voluntary act of a lifetime.

He went around with them, lived from place to place in Pangasinan, and later, as he gained a position of leadership, he went from province to province in the northern Philippines wherever there was a call or need for him for his special skills, characterised by his calm and paternal management style.

He was fortunate to have Ka Pascua as a leader who was a patient teacher and even while he was the youngest of the group, he was treated with respect.

He was their host for several days in his home and they were aware that he had been a member of an anti-rich and indirectly an anti-government group whose reputation was regarded with awe and grudging respect and at times feared in the rural communities. He also knew a lot of people in the barrios from his *colorum* days. These barrio people were elders looked up to by the community.

His recruitment, therefore, boosted the propagation effort

of the group and soon eastern Pangasinan was the beachhead of the sect's push to northern Luzon.

But their leader was careful not to be outwardly deferring to him with the treatment camouflaged as protégé and apprentice. They genuinely regarded him as a prized catch. My father reciprocated by willingly accepting his low standing in the group. The leader put in his mind the biblical saying that those who are humbled will be exalted. The leader's charisma and examples of humility made my father a good follower to the hilt.

He was the gofer, an all-round guy, the obedient acolyte who was asked to go here and there and do this and that for the group's needs. He cooked and washed and ironed the clothes which basically consisted of a white suit or 'de-hilo' type[144] which was a prescribed get-up for the fledging missionaries.

There were none of the underground operations as advance party or lookout during a hit during his anti-government days. He was now a soldier of God carrying the scripture as armament rather than a 'calibre 45'. [145] He appreciated the fact that they did not go on their propagation sorties at night without being properly dressed in their standard 'de-hilo' white suits except for my father, the new recruit and handyman. This manner of attire, the programme prescribed for public expositions like gospel singing and reading which cultivated an aura of spirituality followed a standard procedure which was akin to the ways of Protestant churches, projecting authority in the interpretation of the scriptures.

Felix Manalo, that early in the sect's life, knew how to

---

[144] White linen suit.
[145] Rimless straight-walled handgun which is caliber 45.

deal with men and exploit human psychology. Of course, the success of the church, which defied odds, was ascribed by members as the handiwork of God. Subsequent evangelists inspired by Felix Manalo's feat also succeeded in forming their own sects and this is an eloquent testimony to the peasants' need to feel a sense of security by clinging to something profane even if purveyed by merchants of hope and miracles.

The young assistant had put up with their sense of humour as well to make light of their shortage or lack of resources. This cavalier attitude of their dire circumstances was mistaken by my father as deliberately making him look and feel like a fool.

It happened that for almost three days, they had nothing to eat. The first two days they had to make do with porridge with barely anything solid in it. What they lacked in food, they compensated for with prayers hour after hour with the supplication to God that he moves souls to provide for their needs. But their prayers remained unanswered so that on the third day, their supply of rice completely ran out. When the leader asked him to cook for breakfast, he reported that their supply is gone. The leader gave him a stone which the day before the leader had picked from the river and told him it is good for scrubbing the skin.

"What will I do with it?" he asked.

"Boil it and add some salt."

He complied and after boiling he was asked to serve it as the breakfast for the day.

The leader prayed and everybody was moved to tears as this was interpreted to be inspired by the Holy Spirit. By lunch, the leader asked him again to cook for their meal and he reminded the leader that they have nothing. He asked him for the stone, and he was instructed to boil it once more, this time with more salt. Another moving prayer and the group took the lunch unmindful of the fact that it was a fresh river stone boiled in salted water. This was the time of bygone years when the waters from rivers were still pure, sweet and nourishing.

They prayed that God would provide them with the food they need but my father murmured a wish to have good sleep instead to do away with the gnawing hunger. At night, he was rudely awakened by Ka Pascua, their group leader. He nearly fell from the bamboo bed or *'papag'*[146] posted by the open window which he would not have minded if there was food to eat at that moment. Instead, he was asked the same thing: to boil the precious stone again, but he remained stretched out without any intention to move at all. By the third request, he had summoned his guts to shout back with impertinence to show that he cannot be taken for a fool.

He was now in doubt about remaining in their company and the monster of a rebel in him which had become dormant was coming back.

The leader summoned the group—five of them including my father and led a prayer of supplication for food saying that if their work is God's work, He will send someone to deliver them from their hunger and restore their faith. My father was easily moved and cried the loudest realising his impertinence and also that he had given up hope and was going back to old ways triggered by self-pity. He resolved to leave them the following morning. Why would he be asked to do what is obviously not possible? They would almost hear him talking to himself until he fell asleep.

---

[146] Wooden bedframe usually made of bamboo.

At dawn, he woke up with what he imagined to be the loudest roosters' crow ever because with an empty stomach and weak from hunger, the sound waves become deafening. Before the rooster ended its morning ritual, they heard a young girl's voice outside the small hut. They asked my father to attend to the unexpected guest and when he was at the bamboo stairs, there she was with a big basket with assorted fruits, vegetables, dried fish and rice.

He excitedly reported this manna from heaven to the leader, but the latter instructed my father to politely decline the favour, to his great chagrin. It was a dilemma for my father. He did not immediately convey the unrealistic instruction in the context of their hunger and asked instead to be taken to the girl's father so he could explain the situation. The father of the girl, a respectable and influential Catholic, insisted that his offer was not for anything onerous in return like a way of making them leave the barrio, but my father told him that he can only accept the food if he is allowed to help for a few days in the old man's repairs of his house. Reluctantly, the old man relented.

It was the beginning of a long friendship with that family. They were not converted to the cult and my father did not badger the family on religious issues nor did he exert a kind of friendship to get them to their religious side, but it resulted in lessons learnt for my father for he saw the kinder side of man even in being different.

From then on, my father became more tolerant and open with any person regardless of one's belief and conviction. I often asked him if that family had earned salvation with their kindness even when they were not baptised in the church. He would not judge but to him, it was important to know that when you pray sincerely, it will be answered. This reinforced his faith in God and was the start of completely abandoning violence as a way to correct the misfortunes in life.

He did not leave for home, but that incident made him a man in their estimate and earned him the leader's admiration at the tact he exhibited allowing them to negotiate the impasse without losing face.

*

The following weeks were full of inspired activities around the rural areas where the nights of proselytization were met with enthusiasm by the rural folks. It helped a lot that the members of the group had good voices to sing gospel songs where the children joined as if they were part of the entourage. The Filipino love for music was a common bond among the missionaries and the youth which helped much to soften the resistance of those who did not want to change their faith.

The Catholic churches were mostly in the 'población' or town centre and the priests did not regularly venture to the outlying areas. They practically surrendered the territory to these new evangelists. However, the number of crowds did not necessarily result in a conversion. The Catholic faithful were still numerous and fanatical to the core. The 'Semana Santa' or Holy Week, fiestas and the Christmas seasons were opportune times where the Catholic priests were able to regroup and rekindle the fervour for their religious constituencies so that, despite the almost animistic way these were practised, the old church did not deign to prevent it.

It is ironic that the Catholic Church, which is supposed to be biblical and built on the gospel, survived because it embraced by default its doctrinal antithesis which is a kind of fanaticism akin to paganistic rituals. It is history repeating itself with Constantine the Great harbouring the Christians but appeasing his pagan subjects by adopting their multi-gods, celebrations and holidays like Christmas which was originally a pagan day.

The new evangelists pounded on the idolatry that went with these processions organised by the well-to-do who wanted to show a display of gratitude to saints for their intercession for the bounty they received from God. These frontal attacks antagonised the Catholic devotees. Besides, the ruling class in the areas, the people who were treated with privilege and who felt entitled, who could be depended upon for largesse and financial resources in times of need still belonged to the centuries-old church as well as to the Protestant churches who had financial subsidies from the churches in the United States and Europe.

At the work levels, the new converts were ostracised while at the family level; a son or daughter who became a member of the new sect was disowned and treated as a castaway or non-existent. Persecution and ostracism did not have its intended effect and instead became to the new sect the natural energy that fuelled its growth like sun and water to a plant.

My father dedicated these times to reading the Bible and familiarising himself with the verses which Felix Manalo had used as the anchor of this new Christian faith. It did not take him long to finish reading the entire Bible and with his innate intelligence and intense interest to learn, he was able to commit to memory all the verses needed to defend his new faith. He was now ready to be a regular missionary and was ready to take on the Catholic and Protestant forces who have now realised the threat posed by the new sect.

It helped that those following their religious crusade had gradually increased in numbers and the contributions or 'abuloy'[147] which consisted not only of money but in kind were regularly sustained. The doctrine of voluntary tithing was emphasised as the key to the economic success of the faithful in their personal lives. The missionaries just kept what was needed for their cause and sent the rest to the central office in Manila which was beginning to have the semblance of organised governance.

The church was starting to grow and many of the Ilocanos converted in Pangasinan had left the province for better opportunities in Cagayan Valley, in Manila and in Mindanao. It was also the same pattern among the new converts in the other areas of Central Luzon as well as in the Southern Tagalog region. Many were also assigned to the Visayas in response to the clamour for missionary work of some early adherents in those areas.

The peasant converts expended their energies in their new faith and their individual understanding of this new version of the gospel as the exclusive key to their salvation to the exclusion of those who rejected the message of Felix Manalo, transcended into one of collective strength and solidarity.

Where the revolutionaries failed in the independence movement, Felix Manalo succeeded on the spiritual front by shaping a homegrown religious upstart into a worldwide behemoth.

---

[147] Religious collection during church services.

*

The five-man team where my father belonged was disbanded and each one was assigned to other places in Pangasinan to cope with the expansion of the membership.

He was left behind in Urdaneta and the other adjoining towns where he was able to establish his own team. Now, he is the leader under the supervision of the provincial minister. His old leader became the provincial leader until he was assigned somewhere outside the province. But he did not forget the young man, his acolyte, for whom he gave kind words to his successor and attested to his industry, diligence, intelligence, faith; the experience of faith that turned into a loyalty to the church, and leadership, but above all a developing eloquence which in time will be heard and witnessed across the province. These early leaders of the church did not allow partiality and bias or play favourites among those to be anointed as missionaries, but simply judged from what they observed and felt in their interactions, of the kind of men they needed to handle the missionary work and management of its affairs. Almost to a man, they fitted the bill and the choices made were a key to the unprecedented success of this church.

As a group leader, he developed a confidence to make bold statements as shown later. At that time, the Catholic Church had organised the rural faithful against this persistent and persuasive missionary that every time he would set up to speak in the rural plaza, they discouraged people from attending and listening and even instructed all households to close their houses to show that they were unwelcome.

My father found the Catholic counter-offensive to be a

challenge to the propagation of the faith. Now that he is alone doing this in his assigned area he has to adopt means to deal with the dirty tactics which, for example, were sometimes childish insecurity, as when the windows of the houses being closed at the sight of a gas lamp installed in a corner, a sign that the *'Iglesia ni Manalo'* as they are now called in mockery, will have its missionary meeting which the old leaders during that time called 'propaganda', [148] a word no longer used as its meaning nowadays is associated with trick advertising. It was usually preceded by a day-long house-to-house visits to announce that an evangelical meeting will take place in the evening. Having given notice, the Catholic leaders in the place would conduct their own discreet house-to-house to discourage anyone to attend the meetings. It was a big challenge which at first was usually very successful.

An incident of that kind happened for many evenings where the evangelical meeting was unattended with only my father and two companions forlorn on one street corner. The only thing that they could do was to sing gospel songs, pray and then call it a night. For at least three days, they followed the same process and on the last day, decided to pack up go to another barrio. But my father after the prayers made a final charge and started to address the closed windows assuming that the inhabitants were listening to the prayers and singing. His voice was booming because the night was still, and no soul was on the prowl in the streets. As he went on, he felt that his voice was growing with enthusiasm and could even feel the emotions surging, empowered by his frustration and tenacity to bring the word of God in that area. Then, without any

---

[148] Nightly evangelical exposition in town plaza to generate followers.

premeditation, he began warning the people inside the houses that to prove the truth of his message he would pray to God to make them sick and only his prayers would get them healed.

It was a bold statement that could blast flat into his face. Like a gamble, he put all his bets in that statement with an unmistakable sound of audacity.

Then, the following day when he woke up, he surveyed the place and to his surprise, all the windows were closed even if it was already midday. He went back to his lodging place without making any connection to what he had said the night before as, in fact, he had even forgotten about it.

Then there was a knock at his door and his own assistant came to him and informed him that one of the elders in that street—in fact, the most respected, wanted to talk to him. He was surprised to learn that there were sick in those houses where the windows were closed.

With the old man, he went from house to house and prayed for them in the way the band prayed for him when he was sick and to his surprise, they became active again as if they were never sick before. The entire stretch of that street was converted to his church and that added to the lore about him among his peers and the members of the sect.

When I related this incident to my friends in the canteen one of them asserted that the sickness that befell the barrio folks could have been induced by the emotions generated by the gospel songs and discourse passionately delivered by my father. That is the same line I hear from secular humanists today. But the main adversary, the Catholic priests, would not have invoked this humanist reasoning for that would expose their own history of exploiting the Virgin Mary and the saints as the miraculous cause of any unexplained experience which strengthened people's faith in the Catholic Church.

My father, had he been alive today, would cite the fall of the 'walls of Jericho' as divinely caused after the seven days of chanting by the Israelites and not emotions induced as the walls would not have emotions. He was always ready with biblical references.

# 11
# FELIX MANALO'S CHESS PLAY

The conversion of an entire street has brought my father to a legendary status among the *'cabaguis'*[149] in the province as the members of the new sect were called. In the Tagalog region they addressed themselves as *'kapatid'* or 'brother'. This coincided with the time when Felix Manalo was scanning around and scouting for loyal and committed standouts that could backstop his chosen successor, his son Eraño, who abandoned his dream of becoming a lawyer and became a missionary himself, when the time comes.

There were bright and charismatic associates who were with Ka Felix when he started his mission and whom he saw as having their own agenda and some who had seen him in good and bad times and could exploit his human frailties. They posed a challenge to his leadership, and he suspected them to be behind a national scandal spread on national tabloids. They may even make an attempt on his life which was possible in a country that thirty years earlier was bloodied by a revolution. He was like a chess grandmaster. To win and in his case, for the church he built to fulfill its biblical destiny, he must adroitly plot his next moves.

From the outside, the campaign of the Catholic Church

---

[149] Ilocano word for brother/sister.

against this upstart congregation succeeded to slow its momentum temporarily. Felix Manalo saw this threat and responded.

With the biblical verses, he whipped his flock into a doctrine that dictated to vote as one in any political exercise. It was a master stroke because in time, they gained power and influence and could eventually even dictate the policies of the government. Presidents and high government officials trembled at the mention of the church. The people were jeering at their back for this improper sycophancy although in time begging for the sect's vote became a fashion and the norm.

Felix Manalo brought the level of politics to an 'art of charade'.[150] It brought the members so much pride for they were still small in numbers comparatively speaking yet they were able to parlay their unity in political exercises into a power block although their bigness then was more of a perception rather than a reality.

The Catholic Church sulked at playing a secondary or almost insignificant role in king-making. The opportunity came to show its fangs with the Marcos dictatorship in its death throes. Cardinal Sin riding on a righteous clamour of the people for a right to choose the way to live freely found his voice with the cacophony of old oligarchs. The aftermath left those who formed the bulwark of this civil disobedience watching in disgust at the betrayal of their legitimate cause. The villains of Philippine society who were peons of the church came back to power.

Felix Manalo's instinct for survival is matched only by grandiosity in the building of chapels that did not fail to

---

[150] Politicians begging for votes based on exaggerated number of members.

impress. It was seen by the sect's faithful as a validation that they were God's chosen people, which he claimed was made through a prophecy. But in mortal terms, the infrastructure was both a boost for internal pride for the members who came from the lowest economic rung of the society and magnified a perception of power in terms of resources and unity that begrudged other religious groups.

His eldest son was assigned in the building of chapels whose efficient and strict ways had complemented and faithfully implemented the vision of *'Kapatid na Felix'* in scattering dots of gothic houses of worship in the years to come with efficient and honest use of funds. The eldest child, Ka Pilar, devoted herself in adopting Western Protestant gospel songs to the Filipino longings for a paradise in the other life where there are no more sufferings and afflictions, a theme that captivated all of its adherents. The gospel songs were the emotional glue among the peasants and the new sect, and more importantly a force to make a cult of the founder himself.

Felix Manalo had covered all bases as the saying goes. His sons and daughters were key to his efficient administration of the church which left no stone unturned. He himself was on the way to stardom in the eyes of his flock, which he unquestionably deserved, and his pulpit encouraged it for the glory of God.

Having enough stars on his side, Felix Manalo silently purged the critics among his senior ministers who were themselves household names within the church and were spellbinding speakers, and then reorganised his key advisers. A few stars voluntarily left and started their own sect.

The recruitment of allies by the Manalo detractors was in high gear in Central Luzon, especially in Pampanga. There was also silent proposition in Pangasinan to recruit my father to their side and they told him about the numerous affairs of Felix Manalo and the latter's lust for power. But my father heard none of these. He knew where to place his bet and stuck with Felix Manalo. His unmoved loyalty was based on his faith in the biblical status of Felix Manalo and in hindsight because the sect had already grown, which they concluded as fulfillment of their prophetic readings and that he invested his time and youth in it. His experience had been mostly ascribed as part of that biblical prophecy.

My father has yet to meet Felix Manalo but unknown to him he was already in the latter's wish list among his son Eraño's close circles at the appropriate time.

*

I recall my father's recollection of the first time he came face-to-face with Felix Manalo. This was during the Japanese occupation of the Philippines in World War II. He was twenty-three years old at the start of the war but his experiences from many situations and in dealing with different kinds of people of different beliefs and persuasion made him look mature beyond his age. No one thought that he was barely out of his teens.

Felix Manalo had directed a call for a national meeting in his Manila central office of his provincial leaders to map out new ways in their campaign for members and strategy to protect the sect. This, in light of the fact that the country was already occupied by Japanese soldiers and many checkpoints dotted the national highway to the capital that impede their Thursday and Sunday services.

Then, word came for him to report to the office of the provincial minister in charge of the sect at Dagupan City. He learnt that he was one of two regular missionaries assigned to accompany the provincial minister and sect's treasurer to report to the Manila office for the general conference presided by Felix Manalo. The treasurer was with them to remit the *'abuloy'* from the members collected from its Thursdays and Sundays worships, not only from the province of Pangasinan but also from La Union and the northern provinces.

They had a big problem because there were no motor vehicles available for the trip to Manila and the railroad was under repair or commandeered by the Japanese army for the transport of their soldiers. The Death March was in full swing as well.

So, they had to use the most available means with which they were familiar, the bicycle. The people of Pangasinan are known for their prowess in cycling and my father had once bicycled his way from Urdaneta to Baguio City and back during his younger days. But it would be a perilous journey because of the many Japanese checkpoints where they could be caught in crossfires from attacking anti-Japanese forces. They were carrying a substantial amount of *'abuloys'* which they have to protect with their very lives if needed. These were considered to be sacred as they had been prayed over in a symbolic offering to God for use in propagation of His words.

To avoid suspicion, they split into two groups, and he was assigned to be with the elder. They marked their rendezvous along the way, and these were the houses of those who had been converted in the church. The route covered the provinces of Pangasinan, Tarlac, Pampanga and Bulacan. They were familiar with the houses along the way in Pangasinan but not in Tarlac, Pampanga or Bulacan.

Another missionary who was familiar with the places of members in the province of Tarlac was originally slated to join the trip but two days before departure, he got sick. That was the reason for the abrupt notice given to my father to report to the Dagupan City office. Although my father had been to Tarlac during his *colorum* days six years ago on errands but his previous comrades at arms had been all captured or dead.

The elder decided that he and my father would take the lead and after an hour, the next pair will follow. They also split the *'abuloy'* or contribution into two bags to be carried by each pair to ensure its safety. They would regroup in Tarlac, where there is a big office of the sect and planned to spend the night there. They wanted to cross Pampanga in the daytime because they did not want to have another problem with splinter groups of *hukbalahaps* who were active in the area.

They reached Tarlac. Nothing had happened along the way, except for them meeting many of their members who had been expecting them to pass. Every stop was a group of members who wanted to be prayed over especially because these were uncertain times and the Japanese had shown themselves to be strict and threatening. These meetings were conducted discreetly to avoid being suspected as being anti-Japanese. The members knew the dangers this group of missionaries were taking for the sake of the church and this example of unquestioned reliance on prayers made a singular contribution in galvanising the church's unity and devotion of its members.

The real test in the trip was yet to come though.

The Pampanga portion did not pose any danger at all, so they thought. Pampanga was a bastion of Catholicism, but it was also where the peasants were poorest. Their landlords were favourites of the priests as the rich families were generous donors to the Catholic Church and had encouraged their sons to enter the priesthood. Equally, the sect had attracted in the countryside a good number of peasants who were willing to defend the new faith with their lives. Almost imperceptibly, despite the war, a battle was underway where the dominant Roman church was being challenged for hegemony among the peasants by this upstart sect whose foot soldiers roamed the hinterlands with the charges that the Catholics were superstitious, and the priests engaged in peddling God's favours. The peasants were identifying themselves with the poor but charismatic preachers.

Word had spread in advance that my father's group would be passing that day and spotters were positioned along the route to ensure their safety. But the group did not know about this until later. This way of watching each other had seeped into the culture of the new sect and this was called *'kapatiran'* or 'brotherhood', a trait honoured in earnest which distinguished them from other groups or denominations.

The travel through Bulacan province was uneventful and it was already about midnight when they reached Caloocan, the first town of Rizal province adjoining Manila. Then there was a Japanese post that was unmanned. To their surprise, the Japanese soldiers were on the road lying on their backs, presumably they had been tired and decided to rest and gone to sleep in two rows with their heads next to each other in the middle of the levelled pavement.

There is no other way. They hesitated to cross but sensing the sleep of the Japanese was deep and sound, they started to bike through the opening between the heads of the soldiers.

Luckily there was light from the sentry post and there were at least twenty soldiers, ten each in a row. It was a tense moment while they pedalled enough to keep the wheels running and pass, otherwise with the loss of momentum, their bicycles would fall sideways and cause a reflex action to step on the pavement or on the heads of the sleeping Japanese. They made it through to their great relief and as soon as they passed the last Japanese soldier, they accelerated their speed to safety.

When they arrived in Tayuman Street in Manila where the office was located, the other groups coming from other directions had their own unique account of their journey which they all attributed to God's vindication of their religious mission.

Felix Manalo's summons to the leaders of his sect in dangerous times was a masterstroke.

*

At the general meeting of ministers and missionaries, Felix Manalo presided over the thanksgiving prayer for the safety of his flock. After the meeting, Felix Manalo invited each provincial delegation to private talks in his office and it was here that my father was introduced to the leader.

To my father, this is the second most important audience he would have, the first one being in the cusp of reality and dream. It was in the form of light while bedridden with high fever in the company of his fellow missionaries roaming the villages of Pangasinan. It was when the *Iglesia ni Cristo* was in its infancy. He was the youngest of the group. Noting his grave condition, he was advised to go on sabbatical in his house in Nangcayasan, Urdaneta so he can nurse his health back. But he stayed with them and on the third night, his fever reached critical level. They prayed for him in what they call *'culto de oracion'* applying sacred oil, so called because it was prayed over, on his limbs and upper extremities. In earnest, he asked for a sign that he was on the right path. He either lost consciousness or he fell naturally into deep sleep but in the middle of the night he was awakened by the brightest light ever blinding him even with his eyes closed. Then, when he opened his eyes, he saw Christ bathed in light in full glory. It was the holiest face he could imagine, and he was so humbled that he felt unworthy even to see it.

In the morning, his fever subsided and when he confided his experience the night before no one made any comment, suggestion or interpretation. He knew it was too real to be a mere hallucination and as such it was the attestation of the holy spirit on his new calling.

That spiritual experience connected him to a transcendental power that made his talks about God and the church's gospel ring with truth and sincerity. It was not uncommon that a congregation in a worship service of the fledging church should lose themselves in the cleansing air of spiritual hysteria that goes with his presence. Many of the old converts who witnessed this phenomenon — not only with my father but among the early ministers of the church as well — are wondering why this is hardly experienced now in the modern era of a wealthy, powerful, worldwide church. Is it akin to a paradise lost or has God's promise to Felix Manalo been withdrawn?

With Felix Manalo's sixth sense, he may have felt the aura exuded by the young man. He welcomed my father with a warm handshake and an affectionate pat on the back.

# 12
# TO BE OR NOT TO BE

The experience on that trip was to him an adventure to the centre of his known world. He had pushed really hard to make it there, from the physical act of cycling during the last few days going to Manila, but pushing hard emotionally, spiritually, and psychologically since he lost his mother. Having seen Felix Manalo in person and talked to him, no matter how briefly, the aura and energy he felt in his presence cemented my father's belief that Felix Manalo was the last messenger of God.

Felix Manalo had explained in that meeting that the occurrence of this big war, after a brief interval of about two decades since the First World War in 1914, was the signal of the end of time described by the prophet Isaiah at which time the last messenger of God would rise from the East according to prophecy. In the sect's conversation, he is the messenger.

The spiritual experience of sitting so close to the flesh of the last messenger of God was too powerful and moving. My father forgot that for the hours and days of cycling towards the central office in Manila from Pangasinan, he had keenly anticipated the prize of meeting him, and the relief from almost impossible deliverance from the real perils along the way of that travel, like traversing a row of heads of Japanese soldiers, escaping unscathed, partly fuelled this enchantment. In his mind, he had been elevated to being a disciple of this charismatic man, a reasoning more linked to emotions rather than logic.

The groundswell of emotion could have easily led an ordinary rural folk to the point of no retreat in embracing the great man's evangelical work, a plunge that is both blind and unquestioning. But this is not a case for my father. Instead, when the euphoria of that first meeting had died down, he fell into ennui that dug deeper into his psyche and to revitalise himself, he started to re-examine the course that he had taken in his life.

*

In his adolescence, he had defied authorities, committed many sins in the lost lives and the properties destroyed during their campaign for justice. Now that he was preaching what God forbids, the guilt was coming back to him. He was bothered by the hypocrisy of it all, and it made him feel unworthy of this calling. As he reflected, he felt naked and gross before God. His conscience ruled over his emotions. He felt unworthy to even hold a Bible.

He woke up in the deep of the night perspiring, not because of the summer heat which was made pleasant enough by the sea breeze blowing undisturbed into the open windows of his hut. It was this dream, which was almost real, that almost convinced him that he saw an old man in the deep part of the sea sinking and groping for air and wildly trying to stay afloat. His instinct was to swim to the old man's rescue, but the tide engulfed him, and my father was frustrated knowing that the old man was still there and could have been saved from drowning had he not woken up.

The dream reminded him of the life he had led before he met this band of evangelists. He had wanted to be relevant and useful to the plight of the disadvantaged, the victims of injustice, and those considered social outcasts. In short, he has to deal with the needs of the world now instead of using the gospel of the Bible to focus on a beautiful afterlife.

Obviously, he was finally liberated from the hypnotic spell of these Bible-trotting men who entered his life in his adolescent age. All their faces flashed before him in his thoughts like a series of portraits on a computer monitor these days. He visualised their faces, again and again, searching for a clue of malice or avarice in bringing him to their side and who among them perpetrated that subtle ritual of brainwashing and therefore the most to blame. His mind alternated from rage to simple displeasure to an ambivalent feeling of guilt that he may be unreasonably accusing them falsely. He did not feel a sleight of hand in their dealing with him and he felt a sustaining goodwill from the confidence, trust and the psychic rewards of fulfilment from the joint work of evangelising nights with them. Yes, he could have argued with them that they were manipulating the ignorance and vulnerable circumstance of the people in the rural areas by selling them a hope to see a city paved with gold, where there will be no more suffering, and this will definitely happen in a future reincarnation like Lazarus rising from the dead.

His frustration that he abandoned an earthlier life dedicated to correct social injustice in his present world and that innate feeling of coming to the rescue of anyone aggrieved overwhelmed him. His life was to be a soldier to fight injustice; in this life now, had been side-tracked by these men to take a road still unseen. There was some madness or even something messianic in his longings to confront the evildoers of the present world, but he felt phoney that he was drawn to save man's soul by propagating the idea of an afterlife in bliss through inspired words picturing a heavenly place where only the good prevails. His reasons belong to the first, but his faith urged him to profess the other.

He decided to go to the San Fabian shore about two hundred metres away, where the sound of the sea was louder, to still the conflicting voices from within himself.

*

San Fabian is the northwest side of Pangasinan along the vast China seas and across the horizon is Vietnam and China. San Fabian is like a halfway station where his great-grandfather and clansmen had disembarked from their makeshift boat called *'paraw'*,[151] which was good enough to transport their belongings and other useful tools they could load from the coastline of the Ilocos proper in search of a better life in the central plains. Their direct forbears had settled in Urdaneta, a town eastward, which at that time was already the crossroads between the commercial town of Dagupan to the west, La Union to the north and Baguio City to the northeast. His great-grandfather prospered and acquired a respectable size of landholdings in Nangcayasan, a barrio south of the town proper. The landholdings were substantially reduced by the carefree life of his Uncle Rico and so only his father's inheritance consisting of sugar and rice land was left as a tell-

---

[151] Small traditional boat with a sail and two bamboo outriggers.

tale sign of past hard work. Even that would have been lost to usurers, but my father's quick understanding of the situation prompted him to go straight to the moneylender where he made a strong pitch which was both pleasant and veiled with negative consequences. The moneylender relented and as a graceful exit, my father gave him some honest work for at least a month to allow him to act as not giving in to the young man. Now, San Fabian is likewise his halfway house to ponder his next steps.

The bicycle, his means of transport during these war times, was just parked on the foot of the bamboo stairs and waiting to be mounted for the short trip to the seashore but he decided instead to walk barefoot. The Japanese sentry along the way ignored my father as he saw him sobbing because of his mixed emotions, assuming him to be harmless and not a threat to their security. His was actually a familiar face in the vicinity, and they knew him to be the Bible-toting guy that is seen going to homes to preach. Actually, the Japanese sentry was of Korean descent, who had told him that during this war Korea and Japan are actually one country. When I was reading the story of the World War II Japanese occupation of the Philippines, my father told me that it was the Korean soldiers in the Japanese army who committed most of the atrocities and he reasoned to me that this was their way of showing their frustration and disgust at the Japanese occupation of their country. He was vivid in his recollection made significant by the memory of that night when he was bracing to confront his dilemma.

He must have been in a trance. He walked farther to the shore and to the seawater until he was waist-deep. But the seawater was warm in the wee hours of the morning, and he walked on as if he was transfixed by the cries of an old man gasping for breath. He just walked on deeper, but he could not move farther and faster to save the old man because he himself did not know how to swim. This made him realise that there are limits in his capacity to be the protector of those in need as he came to the humble resignation that there was more he had to learn about himself.

As he laughed at himself, there was a surge of exhilaration in his mood aided somewhat by the curative effect of the morning breeze and salty scent of the sea. It was too soon for him to play safe. His next step forward brought him to the deep that when his feet did not touch the sandy bottom, he instinctively began to swim, but he did not know how to float, and the gravity brought him down. He gasped for air, his spirit breaking out of his body and while the old man was completely submerged, he saw his mother praying before an altar surrounded by priests and when his mother tried to save him, the priests prevented her from fulfilling her motherly instinct. He heard the priests say that her work is to pray and not to save mankind in the present world.

He found himself later lying alone on the shore. The experience made him averse to deep water for the rest of his life.

There were fishermen nearby unloading their catch of fish from their 'banca'[152] which had fished all the way as far as Recto Bank in the Philippines' exclusive economic zone. No one bothered to come to him as life moved in him when he struggled to sit down. Two Japanese soldiers who appeared to have just emerged from swimming were just looking at him,

---

[152] Small boat.

but they did not try to communicate. It was just as well because all he wanted at that moment while the sun started to show itself was to reflect the light in his consciousness of the things he must do from then on.

He was rewarded.

The sun rose at unusual speed during that early June morning, and it did not take long for his shadow to be reflected on the sand and he thought it was darker and bigger than him. Having just been saved from drowning, he waxed poetic and recalled what he had read in the book of Psalms that 'he who dwells in the shelter of the Most-High shall rest in the shadow of the Almighty'. It quelled the tide of torment in him that even the rising sun has a non-verbal way to tell him through the shadow that he could trust in God to guide him on the choice of career he has to make.

He prayed for guidance.

*

At noon the following day, he had a visitor who was unlikely to come but not totally unexpected either. It has often been said that we make an easy scapegoat for our misfortune of those closest to us. Of all his elders in the ministry, he has been a personal advisor, and if he had to regret what he had undergone the last five years, it is he who he will blame the most. But Ka Pascua did not fall in that category. Ten years his senior, he listened to him, allowed an argument or two or exchange of ideas every now and then. He was never hoity-toity. He had guided him and advised him all those years. They were good, exciting years.

The day before, a Tuesday, when he'd almost drowned, he

did not attend the weekly regular meeting and Bible study of all the ministers and volunteer evangelists of Pangasinan in Dagupan City. He had sent word that he was indisposed and as a rule, it is only in extreme cases of a physical disability that failure to attend the Bible study and meeting is excused, otherwise it is considered a serious infraction and grounds for possible dismissal. He had decided to think things over and went to the town of San Fabian in a barrio by the beach for privacy and flight of thought. He was prepared to accept the consequences. He was surprised that Ka Pascua would find him there the following day.

He had learnt to respect this man whose paternal words had calmed him in many situations. He was what my father needed in this hour of deep and painful indecision. This time, however, he was prepared to meet him on his terms fully assured that his mental conditioning is no longer to be a passive and obedient subordinate to this extremely pious elder. He had gathered his wits in anticipation of an ascendant talk from him. He will tell him that the afterlife as a doctrinaire is dishonest without enhancing the immediate value of man in the present life.

After pleasantries, the talk drifted to the incident when he almost drowned. He learnt that two Japanese, one a civilian while the other is a soldier, who were doing their swimming practices had taken him to the shore and resuscitated him. He told Ka Pascua that some Japanese had been in Dagupan City before the Japanese occupied the Philippines and although they believed in God, they were devoted to their emperor.

Ka Pascua observed that in a time of crisis like war, people had to anchor their security in someone or something and to the Japanese, the emperor is their rallying point.

"Right now," he said, "God is our anchor."

My father was impressed even more, and that kind of talk is what made him close to this elder and it has sustained him during the last five years.

"You are twenty-four years old, but you have matured beyond your age!" Ka Pascua turned to another topic which caught my father off balance. He may have noticed that my father was listless and slightly ruffled.

"It is time that you marry and manage a household. A good husband and family man makes a good minister of the flock," He spoke in a manner that was piquant. There was no reference to or rebuke of his absence in the Tuesday meeting.

Ka Pascua stated simply and clearly the sect's rationale in allowing its ministers to marry.

My father did not take offence when Ka Pascua was smiling. What he heard resonated with my father because it showed that his present well-being was important to the church as well. The remark showed that the church also cares for the living and not only about the afterlife. To my father, religion must be an instrument to make a person live peacefully, happily and in an orderly way, not only for himself but for others. He was preoccupied with this notion in thoughts and deeds before he joined the ministry. Now, Ka Pascua had reduced to the simplicity of domestic life the conflict that had been eating him to the core these past few days.

The shadows from his recent past were slowly coming back but the images now were different. Instead of the hatred against those who are taking advantage of the ignorance and poverty of people, he could now hear the endearing and teasing laughter of female comrades during the days that they played hide-and-seek with government forces who were after the radical band of reformists. There were adoring eyes thrown his way during nights of singing and dancing around campfires where there was no fighting. He savoured them. There was joy in innocence. He played the guitar and had a pleasant voice, a musicality that is endemic to the clan. His grandson, my son, even composed a ballad entitled 'Gitara'[153] that became a hit in the country popularised by the band 'Parokya Ni Edgar' which until now is a popular ditty among the youth. His cousins, when they lost their lands to the *'usurero'*[154] even organised a well-sought orchestra that roamed around the eastern part of Pangasinan during town fiestas and other festivities to earn a living. At times, he had been a member of the musical group which was also a cover for his radical activities.

He lost communications with his female comrades when the armed reformists were scuttled by the government forces.

Ka Pascua sounded really serious about marriage as a necessity at least for my father, but he was not prepared for that kind of talk. He had prepared to raise a doctrinal issue on the emphasis on heaven rather than a heavenly life that can be established here and now. The blade that he had sharpened for a verbal skirmish was rendered useless and dull. Marriage is as human an activity like eating, drinking and playing and there is no denying the need for a companion to function better socially, on top of the dictate to go forth and multiply. What he left out is the responsibility and burden of marital life which my father had not contemplated before and now it will take time to prepare for it under the circumstances. To provide for

---

[153] Guitar.

[154] Usurer or loan sharks.

a wife and eventual family, he may have to leave the ministry. Ka Pascua added a new twist to my father's dilemma.

For Ka Pascua, he succeeded in bringing out the demons in my father's mind about a worldly desire which would be better kept in private thoughts. He knows that this is central in any young man at this age which was not lost to my father who realised that the passion of youth had not died in him; that he is a slave to a 'mad and furious master'.

Ka Pascua waited for my father to respond.

Looking out of the open window of the hut, my father saw boys and girls who were half-naked playing and running after another. They were carefree and the Japanese sentry appeared amused as the children were playing a shooting game against each other even as they portrayed a Filipino soldier prevailing over the Japanese. It reminded him of the news of Japanese cruelty in the recent Death March from Bataan after the surrender of the U.S.-Filipino army who were shot or deprived of water and food and left to die in the march like the children mock-shooting at each other. One of his cousins died in the Death March.

"What if I marry the devil's daughter?" my father asked in a hypothetical way. It was a slip of tongue because the inhuman acts of the Japanese at the Death March as the handiwork of the devil entered his thoughts at the same time.

Ka Pascua miscalculated that my father was trying to be smart, and he had to put him in his place. He had been extra careful in his words until then because he knew my father's sensitivity caused him to react with righteous indignation. He did not want to be disrespected if the flow turned sour with a reckless statement. He had to handle the next verbal exchanges like walking on thin ice because this young man will be an asset and he wanted to keep him for the future of the church.

He was visibly irritated because he thought that it was an impertinent question. He did not know that my father was thinking of the children who are playing yet oblivious of a bleak future with the war going on. They could be his children and his responsibility.

"If you think there is a perfect marriage, there is. It is a deaf man marrying a blind woman."

Ka Pascua was attempting humour but it sounded sarcastic because he was visibly irked. My father did not buy his feeble attempt.

"The devil's daughter is entitled to commit a mistake!" Ka Pascua dropped the fatherly veneer and suddenly sounded trenchant which offended my father.

He thought that his ability to be a responsible married man had been challenged, a truth nonetheless that sank deep to hurt him.

"I mean you convert the daughter's father because you have converted a multitude of people before who had been repulsive but with the grace of God you prevailed!"

It was a quick follow-up to recover and maintain goodwill which had been very effective with my father in the course of the talk. He recalled my father's successes in his missionary work. He hoped that this tack would tilt the talk back to his control.

There was a long silence before my father talked.

"Sir, if you think I am breaking from the ministry because of a woman, that is not accurate. I just don't want to be the instrument of deceiving people by making them feel hopeless and the only alternative is to have a place in heaven. I believe in God, and I believe in heaven, but at least they should be delivered from the hell of their present existence. This is what I want to talk about with you!"

Ka Pascua realised he committed a faux pas.[155] He was there upon the instruction of the provincial minister, who may also have received instructions from the church central office in Manila. Felix Manalo had earlier tasked his key people to be all eyes on a list of future church leaders to meet the growth of the church. Many decades later, when the church celebrated its centennial year in 2014, Felix Manalo's right choice of people was prescient with the spread of his ministry all over the world.

Ralph Waldo Emerson[156] was right. 'A great institution is the lengthening shadow of a man.'

"Let us first pray," is all Ka Pascua could muster to say.

He knew that his visit had failed and before he left, he asked my father to preside over church services and visit church members in San Fabian, Manaoag and Binalonan, three adjoining towns in Pangasinan, for the rest of the week. My father accepted the assignment at least for another week; his last acts before finally leaving the ministry.

Ka Pascua's resignation to losing a true warrior showed in his drooping shoulders as he went down the bamboo stairs of the hut. He correctly guessed that only a tiny thread or just the call of the spirit kept my father attached to their ministry and he took the risk by requesting my father to officiate the worship services. It was his last shot.

---

[155] An embarrassing or tactless act in a social situation.
[156] Most widely known man of letters in America and an advocate of social reforms.

*

My father rose early the following morning thinking of Ka Pascua, whose dejected demeanour was still a faint shadow going down the stairs of his hut. By now he knew that his beloved elder was burdened by the prospect of losing him. He cannot make a decision to leave the ministry yet because he did not want to lose a father figure — a source of strength and his life's anchor. He learnt from him that a blessed life just ensues in the course of a man's pursuit of a noble cause, and a man who earlier lived an undesirable life as he did and be suddenly blessed, the unworthy feeling would hit him like an aftershock. Implicit in that is to be unselfish in one's actions without regard for one's safety or interest in favour of something more significant or greater than his.

The totality of his experience was telling him that Ka Pascua was only clarifying the transition from his past and present life. As he had sensed what my father wanted to accomplish outside the ministry, he explained that a desire is a function of the mind which has no limits, like the freedom to dream of many things or ideas, but to act in pursuit of the dream is subject to the limitation of time and space, of gravity and velocity, and definitely of the laws of nature. To think is to the mind with its unlimited freedom but the experience is a function of material reality, and the range of action is limited.

"Alone you cannot change this world!" Ka Pascua's remark hit bullseye on his quixotic aspirations.

He warned him not to rely upon or blame the stars, or

Clotho, Lachesis or Atropos[157] when his experience brings him pain or life seems to be cruel and success elusive. He reminded my father of the saying that even a soothsayer privately laughs when he sees another soothsayer being consulted by men.

"Even fate smiles if you are foolhardy because you learn from the experience," were Ka Pascua's parting words.

My father did not realise then that it was a swansong from the man who had planted the root of peace and hope and practical reality in his heart. He never saw this unschooled but learned man again after that, but he lived on in his actions, nonetheless.

A marriage as suggested by Ka Pascua was a tempting direction. But all the female companions he had known in the past were all out of his touch, the proposition is will-o'-the-wisp. Nevertheless, he decided to dress up and for the first time, he was choosy about the kind of shirt he would wear although the choice was limited to only three shirts. He groomed with deliberate effort and not the usual perfunctory manner, applied an oily wax on his hair, and suddenly inhaled deeply to check that his breath didn't smell, but then his exhalation turned into a sigh.

He amused himself with his image in the mirror smiling back at him again and again. It gave him relief from the thoughts temporarily unburdened.

The twinkling of his eyes took over. His gaze followed two love birds playing a catch-up game and then settling in a mango tree laden with ripe fruits in his neighbour's back yard.

---

[157] The three fates in Greek mythology: Clotho — the spinning fate; Lachesis — the one who assigns to man his fate; Atropos — the fate that cannot be avoided.

Thinking of a dozen ripe mango fruit as a gift betrayed a clumsy romantic who would yet learn a flower as a better expression. And realising that there is no one to accept his token was giving him an ataxia attack.

It was a déjà vu feeling. He remembered his doting mother had called him 'Kismet' after an incident when he went to her with bruised arms and a sprained ankle. His mother knew that the childish hell he was suffering was the result of his good intention.

He clearly remembered a bunch of five ripe and round guava fruits dangling attractively at the end of one of the higher branches. A twist of a long pole with a split end can easily bring them down but he dismissed that option. He had been obsessed by the beauty of the bunch which he watched grow to that grandeur with a daily vigil with his time and patience starting the day he discovered them. The unity of an almost perfect and delicate ripened skin and the sweetness it represented had been reserved for the first person he loved: his mother.

It may just be a strange coincidence that the same gusto fixed on three big chico[158] fruits possessed my wife when she was conceiving my eldest son, and when some playful kids stole the fruits away, my wife's aberrant reaction nearly lost the son who became my father's namesake. This is what the oriental people call 'lihi', [159] the phenomenon that explains why a child would be formed or will behave in the way the thing or experience had dominated a conceiving woman's peculiar behaviour.

---

[158] Brown sweet fruits native to the Philippines.

[159] Infanticipating or craving of a pregnant woman.

He knew that the guava tree was pliable and sturdy. From the trunk, which he scaled easily, he made it to the branch and crawled carefully to the end for his prey. The smell of sweetness teased him to go headlong for the fruits throwing the centre of his gravity off the branch, his hands holding on the fragile guava twigs, and he went directly five feet down.

"Oh, my child!" his mother cried from the distance, but he did not hear her. He kept his feet firmly ahead of his body and as he hit the ground, he fell feet first but tumbled on his back to lighten the impact. It foreshadowed his life.

"Kismet!" his mother recalled telling herself when he saw my father drop on a mound of dried leaves. As he was on his back momentarily, the bunch of fruits with the leaves around it intact, fell on his belly.

His mother was extremely delighted by his son's loving thought, yet it was a foolish and careless act of him to climb a tree in the neighbour's back yard. She sent him to Uncle Rico to apologise and after he explained to him the circumstances, he brought my father back home and talked with his mother. Uncle Rico thought it heart-warming for the boy to surprise his mother with a unique gift which is not a chimera but a real thing with the scent of ripeness only an unrushed time of maturity can process. He even anticipated the smile of surprised glee on his mother's sickly face. That it did not turn into tragedy, they both agreed that my father is a child of fate. *Kismet!*

As my father recalled this event, the pathos was unmistakable as if his mother's mental image were there in a cusp of a delicate balance of pain and smile, a facial expression which only a mother can show when her child is in trouble. How I wished I had stolen that image of his mother from him, to perpetuate it, the way Da Vinci's portrait of Mona Lisa, languished in a dark corner of a museum, but when it was stolen it was so missed, creating a lore about its beauty to earn a place in the pantheon of art. To my father, my grandmother's half-smile and half concern were like Mona Lisa's.

The love birds continued to pursue each other, and my father heard them chirping, *"Kismet, Kismet,"* as if they were privy to his mother calling him that name, beckoning him to go for the fruits of the mango tree. He flirted with the idea that his mother was telling him that it was time to look for someone who deserves a bouquet of flowers or fruits from him. But he did not want to fall from a tree again.

My father wanted to run away from Ka Pascua, but he found he could not get away from one who exists in thought. Then, he recalled Jesus' miracles of the wine and fish in the marriage at Cana.

*Ka Pascua was not urging me to marry. He was telling me about the miracle or signs to guide me to resolve my dilemma. Where is my Cana?*[160] He silently asked himself.

He felt hither and thither!

---

[160] Town in Galilee where Jesus performed his first miracle by changing water into wine.

# 13
# Akiro and the Miracle of Cana

San Fabian is the turning point in my father's decisive choice to continue in his calling as a minister and by coincidence, also the place that gave me a better appreciation of my father's life, a revelation that turned me back to him.

I was about eighteen years old when I went to San Fabian upon the invitation of Manny, who by now had become a friend and confidant. He had actively participated in our last meeting at the canteen. On his own, he went to my place of work to check on the people whom he suspected to have borne grudges when Richie and I had decided to engage in our Binondo business. Port area and Binondo were his reportorial beat thus he had a network of people who gave him tips on business, trade and police matters.

The feedback did not sound good, and he warned me about it. Our reform mindedness had scared a cabal of middlemen serving the needs of vessels in the port area as well as the business establishments themselves that got out of hand. The competition among them in what was a highly lucrative ship maintenance business was fierce and there was the concern that it may deteriorate with the small fries like us getting in the way as collateral damage.

It dovetailed with my Chinese friend's advice to me earlier.

Manny advised me to lie low and, if possible, look for work somewhere else. In the meantime, while the situation cooled at the port area, he invited me to take a two-day trip to Pangasinan where I could both work and sightsee. I accepted.

*

"The charred remains of my grandfather were found here." Manny pointed at a vacant lot with vegetation. "Your father stayed in a hut beside the lot. From the hut he visited my grandfather's house. Then the house was burned, and your father became a fugitive."

Manny related that he was a ten-year-old in 1955 when his grandmother brought him to this house from Isabela. At about the same time, when I was nine years old, my father was reassigned from San Fernando, La Union to Santiago, Isabela. It was turning out that Manny and I were travelling at counterflow from the lowlands to the highlands of Isabela and vice versa.

"There was a vine of pale purple and pink on one side and white flowers on the other over the pergola in front of the house adjoining his hut. The fragrance of that wisteria was sensational when it was in full bloom in May although in June there was still enough to please the senses. My grandfather told me that your father went to this garden and the house to escape from Ka Pascua."

I imagine my father was walking under the pergola. He had told me when I was young about a Japanese whom he had met in San Fabian with a house surrounded by a Japanese garden. The Japanese constructed the house after meeting a Filipina from Dagupan City. They decided to live in San

Fabian where they had some fishing boats which offered the young men there the chance to work as fishermen. He introduced the local folk to Japanese cuisine like sashimi, [161] uni, [162] and salad from the vegetable farm at the back of the house.

Before the start of the Japanese occupation, this Japanese set up a free school for bonsai[163] culture which attracted many of the prominent people, not only in San Fabian but in nearby Dagupan City as well. At first, he was well-liked but when the atrocities that occurred on the Death March[164] filtered into the town, many started to shy away from him. There were those who made a friend of him especially the Chinese merchants and commonwealth local officials who needed to connect with the Japanese command in Dagupan City but to their disappointment, he remained apolitical. Japanese officers found his kitchen well-supplied with fresh vegetables and the catch of the day. Their fondness for his pretty daughter and their regular visits brought chagrin to his wife.

I surmised that the pretty daughter was Manny's mother because of his Japanese features, especially his eyes but not his brown complexion burned by the years under the scorching sun of Cagayan Valley.

Manny was almost teary-eyed when he talked about his family.

"My grandmother and my mother had suffered during the

---

[161] Thinly sliced raw meat or fish.

[162] Japanese sea urchin. Locals call it Maratantang.

[163] Japanese art form producing in containers small trees that mimic the shape and scale of full-sized trees.

[164] A forced march of prisoners of war in which individuals are left to die along the way.

war in a different battle fought at another level. On that battlefield, most of which is mental, she bore the brunt of the ire of the local folks who showed it with dagger looks and swearing at her back. This broke my grandmother's spirit; at first a despondency, then a prolonged depression, until she was thought to be totally out of her mind. There is unforgiving viciousness even from the non-combatants who were physically inured from the theatre of fighting. Even their decency and community decorum were not spared by this senseless war.

"This brought extreme worry to my Japanese grandfather and their daughter, who was seventeen years old, and sadness to their home. The flowers in the garden and the bountiful harvest of his vegetable farm and fishing boats all year round only mitigated these sad circumstances."

As my father walked deeper into the pergola, [165] he admired the green thumb of the Japanese man, Manny's grandfather. There is a shrub of broad-leaf evergreen camellias, azaleas, roses, carmine red dahlias, and orchids. They were basking in the light of the sun in an oasis undisturbed by war. My father was infatuated with plants and a life with nature which was a legacy from his own father. In this beautiful surrounding, my father may have forgotten himself and Ka Pascua.

My father kept a book entitled Glossary of Thoughts which contained quotations and aphorisms and pearls of wisdom compiled through the ages. On the back page, my father wrote this quote: "In the language of flowers, the yellow

---

[165] A structure with posts or pillars supporting cross beams forming a shaded walkway or sitting area.

rose means friendship, the red rose means love, and the orchid means business."

He told me that he heard it for the first time from a Japanese who expressed the quote in Ilocano. He must have been referring to Manny's Japanese grandfather. My father remembered the Japanese telling him those words while he was admiring the plants and flowers but did not correctly guess that he was a Japanese until he bowed in greeting, and he bowed back.

My father recalled that meeting.

"Akiro," he introduced himself.

"Kismet," my father said in return.

"I like your name Kismet-san," he said. "In Arabic, it means 'fate'."

"No, it is not my actual name, but my mother called me Kismet after I survived an accident. I am using it for now. I hope to survive this war," my father explained.

"There is no death in my garden. There is only passing from one door to another. The flowers and the insects, the butterflies, the birds over there, are lives from one form to another."

Akiro-san gestured, inviting him to move forward to the front door of the house. He could hear a piano playing 'Spring Waltz' which he knew by heart. He used to play it on his guitar when he was in his teens.

He told Akiro-san that he was there to thank him for saving him from drowning the other day. Akiro-san bowed to accept his gesture and he bowed back.

Inside the house, the music was non-stop. "I heard that you pray to heal?" Akiro-san interrupted his thoughts. He was taken aback by the oblique request to heal his wife. This time he was not sure he could do it, but he did not want to displease his host who had saved him from drowning. The medical doctors in Dagupan City and the adjoining town whom they consulted had raised their hands, giving up on his wife. It did not help that Akiro-san was not fond of Western prescriptions, and so he made some tea from the flowers in his garden that temporarily calmed his wife and consequently, she began to have moments of lucidity.

"She is not sick!" my father told Akiro-san. The Japanese looked at him bewildered and my father himself was surprised with what he said and even his nonchalance. Surely, there was no providence involved because it flashed back to him that he was no stranger to the wife's phenomenon. Among the fugitives in the mountains or in remote villages, he saw his female comrades temporarily lost their bearings and then came back to their good old selves.

A female face had momentarily come to view when the bedroom door at the far end of the family room opened halfway but closed instantaneously afterwards. My father thought that the face was familiar but could not immediately recall who it might be from his past. There was not enough time to make the recognition and although Akiro-san was quick to notice my father's body language, he decided to keep a beady eye on him.

Instead, my father felt an urge to play the guitar like the old times.

"May I play your guitar?"

He waited for the record player to stop.

Meanwhile, the Japanese in his stammering Ilocano told him that a faith healer had prescribed music to be played non-stop as therapy which he found to be consistent with my father's request. Before that, they had made a pilgrimage to the miraculous virgin in Manaoag church for intercession. His wife was calmed by the hymns sung in the liturgy but after worship, on the way home her unusual behaviour came back.

*

The thing about the faith healer and the devotion of the sick to the miraculous lady is part of the unique microcosm of a place that is so rained with a variety of healing practices or protocols whether natural, superstitious, faith, scientific or medical, or psychic and spirit healing, which the province of Pangasinan is known for. No less than the first civilian governor of the province was himself a faith healer. The towns of San Fabian, Manaoag, Urdaneta, and Binalonan are the centre of the gravitational forces that cemented the province's importance as a 'healing capital of the Philippines' and perhaps of the world. There is an apocryphal account of the lost land of Mu[166] that straddles on the Pacific side of America which was lost and the same way that the lost land of Atlantis had once existed but had disappeared as well. In the town of Anda, anthropologists found fossil bones of elephants which supported their idea that the Philippines was once connected to mainland Asia. In Tambac island, a fossilised fish was found in 1975 which the American scientist Dr Harry Fierstine, a world authority on this vertebrate called a 'marlin billfish fossil' which the California scientist dated as two or three million years old. According to Dr Araneta, he brought some mediums to his farm where the fossils were discovered, and

---

[166] Legendary lost continent of Lemuria.

they said in a trance that it was "a magical fish on which rode the first people of the world. The first people were destroyed by the gigantic eruption, resulting in the sinking of the landmass or continent. On the magical fish rode a certain noble."

This could be a fantasy that exists in the fertile imagination of those who believed that Pangasinan or the Island of Luzon for that matter is a remnant of the lost Mu. However, it is a fantasy built on tell-tale signs like bones and fossils which were discovered in the province.

The accounts of successful healings in Pangasinan brought about mistaken notoriety, at least to the unimpressed scientific community who demand but are slow to conduct rigorous scrutiny. People who believed are righteously indignant. People's attitudes, in general, however, are blasé. While the divergent Christian sects and denominations quarrel on the rightness of their respective faith, the healing zone of the psychic and spirit healers seemed to be a neutral territory because when all scientific or medical avenues are futile, the terminally sick go to them as a last resort. The shrine of the Miraculous Lady of Manaoag is housed in a Catholic dome but it performs as a faith-healing centre as well.

The attention of the world and the recognition of the healing phenomenon, particularly the scientific community, had been sought by the establishment of the Philippine Society for Psychical Research notably by Dr Jesus B. Lava, a medical practitioner but whose prominence rose as one of the founders of the 'Communist Party of the Philippines' and Dr Antonio S. Araneta who is a Doctor of Philosophy from the University of Oxford, England and the husband of the first Miss

International from the Philippines, Miss Gemma Cruz, [167] herself an accomplished writer and prominent advocate of the national arts.

The centre had documented successful cases of healing with the use of psychic surgery, psychic incision, magnetic healing that involved the transference and application of energy from healer to the patient. No less than the late President Ferdinand Marcos attested that he had seen the opening of the stomach of a person without any instrument.

The Philippine Society for Psychical Research was still decades away in the future from the present Japanese occupation in Akiro's and my father's encounter. But the Japanese soldiers who survived the war had attested to the success of these healings and this accounted for the numerous Japanese tourists who came to the Philippines for this unique form of surgery and who had personally experienced their unbelievable cure from their terminal maladies.

Akiro himself had been drawn to Pangasinan in the middle of the 1920s from his place in Kyoto to research this psychic phenomenon but having been enamoured of the rural ambience which suited his minimalist orientation, he decided to stay and make it his home long before there were murmurs of war. He had collected a number of successful cases of psychic healings that made him an admirer of these incredible and gifted healers. He thought that enriching the flora of his adopted country would please the 'energy' that made the healings possible. But the war intervened and now he feared a turbulent future before peace could return. This fear pushed the body and soul to spend most of his time in his garden and

---

[167] 1st Filipino and Asian to win the title in 1964.

his bonsai, but the foliage did not protect him from the alienation and hostility linked to the negative emotions generated by the gruesome news of the Death March. The sneaking suspicion of his bloody end grew deeper by the condition of his wife. This negatively affected the natural optimism he needed to deal with the crisis.

\*

Akiro subscribed to the animating value of music to his plants and the psychic healer's suggestion of uninterrupted music to heal his wife found a willing ear. Now, he did not hesitate to hand the guitar to my father who, on the spur of the moment, had asked to play it after seeing his wife emerge briefly from the room.

It was not long after my father was playing the guitar when a female voice was heard singing from the bedroom and then the face my father thought he recognised emerged. It was a beautiful, melodious voice that was correctly timed with every beat of the guitar. My father's growing suspicion that he knew the voice and the one singing made him pour more soul into his guitar music and they accompanied each other harmoniously.

When the lady emerged from the bedroom, it was like the good old times.

"Kismet?"

"Ingga?"

Akiro-san regarded the two with mixed emotions. He had a keen eye for details which was polished by his daily routine with his plants and flowers such that earlier when Ingga's face emerged from the doorway of the bedroom, an eerie feeling swept over him that the two had previously known each other, but he rejected the idea of a black cat. He had suffered enough, and any negative thought is not what he needed. His overriding concern for the well-being of his wife is the great secret to a strong marriage. His yoga exercises in peaceful surroundings, with the robust growth in his garden, cleansed him of pollutive thoughts that gave him the fortitude to fend against the winds of war.

It helped that Akiro heard his wife behind the door singing an Ilocano ditty to the tune of the music played on the guitar. There is no mistaking the blending between the voice and the instrument, the one feeding on the other for high musical effect. It is an eloquent harmony that only a deep friendship can foster. For Ingga to synchronise with the guitar's beat belies a mind lost in deep sleep. She was conscious of everything after all. It was an encouraging development after days of his wife being reticent and withdrawn. His hopelessness has given way to a brighter prospect for Ingga's restored mental health.

Ingga reached for her husband's right hand and held my father's left and after clasping both hands she brought them close to her chest, a single act expressing love for a husband and a long-lost friend. Then she sat down on the wooden chair pulling her husband to sit close by her side. She was weak and exhausted, but she appeared to be in control of her senses and decorum. In the mind of my father, Ingga had not changed these many years, always clear and unmistakable in conveying her inner thoughts and emotions. Both Akiro and my father understood the non-verbal language being spoken by a troubled wife. The meaning of Ingga's gesture and the wavelength they shared assured Akiro who felt a kinship with this new addition to his family. It was as if they had always been friends and that clasping of both hands made him part of a friendship between his wife and the stranger which had started even before he met Ingga. They are, of course, unaware that the script has been written and a tragic end has been sealed.

*

"Tamako, kiss the hand of your uncle," Ingga called for the young pretty lass who was watching the unfolding of a great reunion from the bedroom door.

*"Mano po!"* [168] said the young girl as she held my father's right palm, bent her knees the way devotees genuflect in front of the altar, a traditional act of respect customary to Filipino children in front of their elders or old folks. As the girl came close to my father, he saw a likeness that is a cross of Ingga and another person he had known, and which reminded him of too much pain and loss. Ingga has correctly read his thoughts, but this was no time to open a closed book especially in front of Akiro who by now was enjoying comfort brought by Ingga and Tamako coddling him. Akiro was never happier in his life than at this moment. The loves of his life returned in their home, and he felt exhilarated.

My father was on a rollercoaster ride of emotion. He brought solace to three afflicted souls and even to his own. He had done something of his heart's desire and since the events

---

[168] Filipino gesture of honouring elders by pressing one's forehead on their offered hand. It is specially done to a priest or a bishop as a gesture of respect or subservience.

happened randomly, he surmised a divine hint as to the path he should take from then on. This is the miracle of the marriage of Cana which Ka Pascua came short of telling him, but it was more for him to discern.

But he is still grief-stricken from the memory of his haunted past. It was serendipitous that he was reunited with Ingga from whom he will seek the answer to finally lay to rest his conscience. Then he will start his life anew with a clean slate.

He wanted to talk to her alone, but the situation seemed to have determined that it was not the right time, when a Japanese army jeep came to a halt in front of the house. Dread came over Tamako's face, but Ingga closed her eyes to steel herself, said a little prayer, and then looked straight at her daughter to assure her that she can deal with the situation. She urged her husband to the door and when he emerged from the house, he was already composed. He bowed to the confident and smiling young Japanese officer who had alighted from the vehicle and who bowed in return. Akiro engaged Hiro in pleasantries in Nihonggo as they usually do in his regular visits. While they walked, surrounded by the different colours and fragrances from the shrubs, vines and perennials under the pergola, they talked animatedly about a common interest. Hiro was drawn to the bright flowers and green leaves and the lure of touching them with care contradicts his warlike demeanour. The love of nature softened his martial bearing as if his army is no longer at war.

The casual gait was only momentary when Hiro entered the house and saw my father. Both reacted in their own way with the Japanese returning to a posture of authority while my father shifted on his seat to convey his own welcome to the houseguest to what has been a sort of reunion. The young Japanese officer was calm and obliging unlike the bluster of the coarse foot soldiers he saw going around town. The only sign that this was the first time the two met was the stiffness from both sides, but they immediately recovered when my father extended his hand while the Japanese made the ritualistic salutation that completely put my father at ease. Both were smiling, but the Japanese smiled like almost losing his eyes which reminded him of Ka Pascua. My father thought that the latter's smile fit him well and the effortless way he did it showed intensity and warmth. They made an instant connection.

Hiro has been briefed by Akiro rather sketchily but nonetheless essentially about Ingga's recovery and the role of the music my father played before they were introduced to each other. After a brief introduction, he excused himself from them and went to a room that was always available for him in his meditations.

*

My father hoped to learn from the Japanese a thing or two on the practice of contemplation. How does it differ from his own dedicated prayers called *'ayuno'* which are done in the presence of two or more among his fellow evangelists?

It is a new experience for him and from there he would later postulate that in the human mind's shared spiritual experience, a common platform had evolved in the inner consciousness during the meditation or prayer where they converse with a transcendent power who lies beyond what they can conceive but feel it is there. There seems to be no logic about God, only faith.

Fast forward, I would later probe my father's thoughts.

"Where would that platform be?"

"It is here!" he answered, pointing to his head. "You have to be sincere and doubtless!"

"What do you mean?"

"You must have faith. Faith means that you are not just doing it as if taking chances in case it is true. You have to *believe*."

"How can you connect?"

"It is not physical. The wireless was never conceived before but now it is just a matter of fact. Who knows how many levels of communications there are in the ethereal domain which is humanly inaccessible?"

Akiro was closely observing my father's deportment when Hiro arrived and correctly judged that my father needed enlightening. When the Japanese officer excused himself from the rest after the initial pleasantries with them, Akiro reached for my father's attention. He explains:

"He always comes here to calm his mind. He finds solace in nature and sees in the flowers, plants, and trees around, along with music especially those produced with wind and string instruments as forces that restore his physical and spiritual well-being. This fosters a sincere attitude in his relationship with other people which made him open-minded to metaphysical explanations of life despite being a man of science and a doctor. He considers war as anathema to the way of inner peace—"

"I think he will find in you good company with your music!"

Ingga cut Akiro short!

Ingga looked at Akiro meaningfully as though the latter might say something from which he could not backtrack. It was pointless for Ingga to make it so obvious to him. In due time, such loaded and meaningful exchange between husband and wife will unravel. My father was almost sure that a risky family enterprise is in the works.

"Meditation is a fast way to connect to the divine which inspires a life attitude of doing what is best in the work being done and in fostering better the relationship with others." Akiro moved on.

"Is meditation the way to purify the heart?" My father was talking to himself and not to Akiro. In the back of his mind came the thought from the Bible particularly the sermon on the mount: 'Blessed are the pure in heart for they shall see God'!

Akiro was assured that my father was completely following his talk.

He showed my father how to meditate by sitting in the lotus position[169] as the way to purify, to forget the 'self'. He explained that the self is the flesh, a construct like a container that can be discarded when damaged. As Akiro was moving into position my father imagined him doing *hara-kiri*.[170] He avoided the urge to explore this morbid thought in fairness to Akiro who has just been relieved of his concern about Ingga's well-being.

"The way to connect with the divine is to transcend from any of the world's desires or attachments by forgetting the self," Akiro continued.

---

[169] Cross-legged sitting pose on the floor to calm the mind and prepare oneself for meditation.

[170] Japanese formal way of suicide by cutting stomach with knife.

225

My father recalled one instance when he had not eaten for three days and instead kept on praying with Ka Pascua. Yet they glowed and the peace of mind they felt was so enjoyable that they tolerated their physical wants. Hence, he could relate to Akiro's version of transcendental experience and somehow seized the sense of a passage to another level of understanding about physical needs being ephemeral and as transient as the flesh and so is the uselessness of material things. He wondered that even as the Japanese did not believe in the Bible there was a consistency between what he believed and what my father professed. There is a headspring of all this wisdom and the yearning among different cultures and peoples to connect with this common source is universal, he concluded. It is his uncanny sensitivity to deduce the significance of these events that brought him closer to the choice of career that he had to make.

He kept his eyes fixed on a blanket laid like a floor mat and a sitting pillow where Akiro sat to demonstrate the lotus position. But he was a hunter in his youth and his other senses were absorbing what was going on around him as well. He felt the footsteps of danger approaching on this family after Hiro arrived and who is now closeted in a room supposedly to perform his meditation.

He heard Akiro say something about doing *'taiso'*[171] to strengthen the physical side because the body hosts the mind which in turn works as antennae to capture a continuous hiss, he claims the sound of the universal energy that connects the entire cosmos. My father has yet to know the Big Bang

---

[171] Japanese exercise.

Theory[172] that evolutionists say accounts for that hissing sound that in later years had been a topic between son and father. I remember my father telling me that I was making things too complicated by ascribing the origin of the universe to this theory instead of the biblical story of creation. He cautioned that the enormity of creation cannot be discerned by my small mind and advised that the space around me must be given importance instead. He cracked that we will die before even knowing how many stars are in the sky.

"Life is too short to unlock the mystery of eternity, but you have a lifetime to make your world better!" he counselled.

*

Meanwhile, as my father was self-absorbed from the insights of Akiro's banter about *'taiso'* meditation and the way to the divine, Ingga broke the smokescreen blanketing the morass of activity going on in the household, particularly among Ingga, Tamako and Hiro.

"They are gone!"

It was Ingga speaking from the meditation room. It was not intended for my father since it was voiced like a stage whisper to finally announce the fruition of what had been long-planned. Hiro's military jeep was gone, and it occurred to my father that Tamako was gone as well. The dread on the face of Tamako when Hiro arrived was not fear but apprehension that a planned escape would miscarry with the presence of my

---

[172] Leading explanation how the universe began. It says the universe as we know it started from a small singularity then inflated over the next 13.8 billion years to the cosmos that we know today.

father. Tamako was too young to be pretentious.

Hiro and Tamako succeeded in escaping to the town of Balauan in La Union which was prearranged. They spent some time in the mountains with the guerrillas[173] who took them in after learning of their plight. The guerrillas had also a good use for Hiro who was a doctor and plant scientist who knew herbal medicine that supplemented the lack of pharmaceuticals in the hinterlands. He avoided being part of the combatants with his professed antipathy to the war efforts on both sides which the guerrillas respected. They also spent time discussing the common cause of humanity that makes the war a useless exercise with Hiro.

"The war is like a conflict in a neighbourhood. One party covets the resources of another. The Japanese, the Americans, and the Spaniards all came here motivated by their own interests."

"We are fighting for our freedom. This includes running our own affairs."

Hiro, a good judge of character, thought that these guerrillas would be fighting against each other in due time for petty powers. But he kept his peace, and he would not risk any misunderstanding with the guerrillas. There would be a time and place for that. Tamako would soon give him a son.

The most memorable part of his stay in the guerrillas' hideout was his enlightening talks with another professional, a young lawyer, who had escaped from Bataan. He was almost his age or a little younger but exhibited a keen sense of the history of his country and an animus unique to a person with a

---

[173] Members of a small independent group taking part in irregular fighting typically against larger regular forces.

purpose. There were also talks about Japanese war booty to which Hiro had been made privy before his escape. He and the young guerrilla officer agreed that the pile of gold and currencies could be a resource at the end of the war for the rehabilitation of the country. Their like-mindedness formed the basis of a friendship which had survived even after the war.

*

"There is another hero in the tragic death of my grandfather, Akiro, and this is Tata Abon," Manny interrupted. "He regarded Akiro a hero, a fine accolade to the very person who stole his dream of uniting with his wife Ingga and the chance to enjoy the pattern of happy family life."

Tata Abon considered his role in the escape of Hiro and Tamako as an inescapable duty. Tamako is his daughter with Ingga when, together with my father, they were running from government forces at the instance of landed caciques in Pangasinan. Tata Abon and my father were separated in a sortie of their group in the town of Tayug in Pangasinan where they encountered a government platoon on the outskirts of the town. Tata Abon was wounded, and my father escaped, but before he could reach the safety of the mountain lair where she was staying with her seven-year-old daughter, he got sick with malaria. He took refuge in a house owned by a sympathiser and from there, he was taken to his Urdaneta home. My father felt guilty for not having informed Ingga about what happened to Tata Abon. She later met Akiro. Thinking Tata Abon was already dead, she married Akiro after a lengthy courtship. Akiro knew about Tata Abon so when the latter reappeared in Ingga's life he had more sympathy than feeling aloof and strange. In fact, he regarded him as a family; after all, he was the father of Tamako whom Akiro treated as his natural daughter and the latter in turn loved him as her true father.

Tata Abon was still a fugitive but now he was fighting for a legitimate cause. A man like him never had a respite all his life nor time to seek personal leisure even if he could have. His real comfort came from the times he was able to do this or that for someone in need. His strength came from his solidarity with the intrepid and like-minded few and he considered my father as one of them. Tata Abon's personal goal must have settled with the comfort Ingga and Tamako were presently enjoying, and he considered Akiro as a friend. Hiro's plight gave him another opportunity to do something for someone else.

*

It was Hiro's advocacy that brought him into trouble. Even at the military academy in Japan, he was part of a clandestine group that was against the Japanese war efforts. His contacts in the upper echelons had assigned him to the Philippines to quietly preach their non-violent advocacy and he had the perfect cover as a physician.

When the Japanese intelligence corps discovered how vast the network of the peace advocates had spread in the military, they started to lay a dragnet to snare all the members and their sympathisers. By that time, Hiro had created a network of Japanese military personnel, including an intelligence officer, who tipped him off in time to escape.

Hiro's advocacy which he told the guerrillas included the Philippines gaining independence hijacked by the Americans in the Treaty of Paris[174] in 1896, a move supported by the Filipino ruling class. His guerrilla host had advocated Philippine independence to the chagrin of the USAFFE[175] stragglers who were nestled in the mountains of Zambales. Tata Abon belonged to the pro-independence group who dreamed of having the Philippines liberated even before the return of General Douglas McArthur.[176] The strategy was to limit the war between the Japanese and the Americans which the former bungled by their treatment of the prisoners of war in the Death March. The new independence playbook was a replay of the 1896 independence movement but this time around, hopefully avoiding the Filipino ruling class' betrayal.

The last time Hiro visited Akiro's home, a week prior to their escape, he complained about the thorns of Akiro's potentilla plants at the same time that a new Japanese officer was assigned to take over the northern Luzon command. He was conveying an alarming message. It was a subtle reference to the Japanese general who was clearly in favour of the war effort and had direct contacts with the Japanese war cabinet. On the day of the escape, Hiro would have been arrested for treason by virtue of a warrant earlier signed by the general. After court-martial, a conviction would have been definite and death by firing squad imminent. The Japanese command was scripting a play about the consequences of betrayal in which Hiro would pay dearly. The looming event agitated Akiro's

---

[174] Treaty signed by US and Spain in Paris that ended their war where Spain relinquished all claims of sovereignty over Cuba, Puerto Rico, Guam and the Philippines.

[175] United States Armed Forces in the Far East.

[176] American Five-Star General and Field Marshall of the Philippine Army who played a prominent role in the Pacific theatre during World War II.

household and aggravated Ingga's condition. It was clear to them that they were trapped between two enemies, both of whom regarded *them* as enemies. There was no zone of neutrality and there was no safe place to hide. But they had the time.

Akiro's contact in the camp alerted them of the impending arrest and so they executed the plan post-haste. Tata Abon was enlisted earlier to actually devise and execute the plan of escape. He was hiding in the meditation room that day my father arrived. He had earlier tipped Ingga off about my father staying at the nearby hut. Years had gone by since he last saw him as a teen and now my father seemed to have a good life ahead of him. He resolved to put my father out of harm's way despite the extreme urge to embrace a man who was a part of his struggles. He put his emotions under leash, resisted the urge of embrace and decided against saying hello to my father.

A few hours after the escape, Akiro received an alert that he should also leave. It was discovered that his connection with Hiro was more than their common interest in nature but in political and ideological advocacy which was contrary to the war efforts. Akiro thought that the Japanese internal police could easily catch up with them if they left together. He urged Ingga to leave earlier than planned. He had plans of his own outside of what was agreed upon with Tata Abon. She initially refused but my father convinced her to go as she was complicit with the plans and there was a possibility that she would be taken hostage and threatened with punishment only to make Akiro disclose the whereabouts of Hiro. They left together in the direction of Binalonan in the east. Later, Hiro's military jeep was found abandoned in the boundary of Urdaneta and Villasis town to the south. It was a decoy to throw them off the escape route which was on the far north of Pangasinan on the way to Baguio City. This gave them enough time to catch up with Tamako and Hiro.

My father refused to go with Ingga because he had to officiate at religious services in Binalonan that afternoon, a duty which he had sworn to fulfill earlier in the house. He had finally resolved what he has to do and silently thanked Ka Pascua for his words of wisdom and the miracle that happened in the household.

Ingga knew from his voice that he had made a decision and did not insist, hoping that prayer would be more reassuring than cunning. She remembered the last time Tata Abon and my father left their mountain refuge with the three of them crying and despite the tears in the eyes of the teen, she could see a resolve to fulfill a mission. As she walked away, my father admired the fortitude of this lady and wondered whether she deserved her fate at all.

There were no teary goodbyes. Not with Akiro, not with Tata Abon, and finally, not with Ingga. Who will die this time?

Akiro looked at his face in the mirror and saw one who has disgraced his emperor. He was told that the emperor was also against going to war and may have been under the behest of a war cabinet that felt that Japan had suffered enough humiliation from the foreign powers. But he agreed with Hiro about the uselessness of war and the destruction of his plants, his flowers, nature in general, and his family. Any time now, the imperial police would pick him up and now that Ingga and Tamako were safe with Hiro and Tata Abon, it is time for him to be released from his guilt.

The burnt remains of a man were found in the debris of the house that had been razed by fire. It was concluded that the remains belonged to Hiro whose lineage comes from a samurai class in Japan. It was recorded in his personal file that he did *seppuku*[177] in protest of the war. The report on the affair was never made public to maintain a united front for the Japanese forces and the pursuit of Akiro's family was called off.

*

"I am sorry for your loss," I commiserated with Manny. In a way, it was also the loss of my father who lost a friend in Akiro. In that brief time with him, Akiro had enriched my father's mind. Akiro's garden was my father's canteen. He reached the end of his quest and now he knew his relevance.

The visit to San Fabian has enriched my heritage and gave me a new appreciation of my father's dedication to his ministry. I was a witness of his ministry that gave equal significance to easing the burdens of the flesh as much as the hope of the soul.

The incident quickly spread in the church circles whose members feared for the life of my father. His involvement with the Japanese family as well as Hiro had put the church members in jeopardy of repercussions. My father, who had resolved to stick with the ministry, was reassigned to La Union where he reunited once more with Ingga and Abon. Hiro assumed a Filipino name and after he had acquired the fluency of the Ilocano dialect and after many months under the sun, he was mistaken to be a native-born Filipino. After the war, Ingga returned to San Fabian, sold a portion of her land there and left the front part in memory of Akiro. Nana Ingga with Tata Abon

---

[177] Another term for *hara-kiri*.

and the couple Hiro and Tamako and their son took the long trip to Isabela province where they started a new life.

It was in La Union, where my father met a lass from Binalonan, the youngest sister of a Filipino immigrant in the United States, who, while there, wrote books that made him a famous writer. They were married, had a son but a year later his wife died of fever, which was aggravated by malnutrition. She was the first casualty of my father's hard life in the ministry.

The church provincial hierarchy heard of the tragedy that befell their young protégé who was struggling to raise a son and fulfil his missionary work. They decided to reassign him to eastern Pangasinan where they hoped that he would marry again so he could take care of his personal life before they gave him a bigger responsibility in the administration of the church.

San Manuel, Pangasinan turned out to be a new Bataan where the Japanese made a defensive line en route to the mountain provinces. Here my father was caught in the crossfire between the retreating Japanese soldiers and pursuing guerrilla and American forces. He led the church members in daily prayers for divine protection. He met there the third eldest daughter of a family of six daughters and a son who were the pillars of the San Manuel congregation. After a courtship between daily prayers and war drums, they married and soon, their eldest boy was born.

The good news about the birth of his son sounded pleasing as the hymn the choir was singing before the start of the church service that Sunday morning. It was the lullaby song my father would always sing to me when I was his little infant.

When we left San Fabian, Manny brought a wrapped shell and gave it to me. It was the shell Tata Abon promised to give

235

me on the bus.

"There were two shells found in your father's pocket when he nearly drowned there." Manny was pointing at the seashore. "It was their pact of friendship and brotherhood. One remained with Tata Abon and the other one with your father. Your father asked Tata Abon to give it to you on the bus."

"You mean he knew I was leaving? It was no coincidence that you were in the same bus." I was incredulous.

Manny just gave a meaningful smile making me feel like the last to know.

# PART THREE

# 14
# MY FATHER FINALLY SMILED

When we came back to Manila from San Fabian the threat from the hurting business rivals at the port area was quelled. The church police had laid low.

'Man is what he believes', as Anton Chekhov[178] said. So, I was seething with disappointment when it dawned on me that what I thought as a life of a gladiator in the wild was actually partly managed. Later when I watched *The Truman Show*, [179] I imagined myself in his place.

All the events that transpired from my escape, my trip to the hospital, the cramped bed space, the hunger on a shoestring budget, the danger in the port area and Binondo, were tainted with the haunted feeling of having dishonoured my father. Now it looked like all that was a charade; in fact, I was living with a parachute to ensure a soft landing, which I realised after uncovering that Manny was sent by my father as my guardian angel.

I felt deprived of the authenticity of a rare life's adventure.

It was the first time my friends in the canteen saw me livid.

---

[178] Russian playwright considered to be among the greatest writers of short fiction in history.

[179] A movie about a man whose entire life is a TV show, and his family members are mere actors.

"Do not complain because everything happens through necessity", remarked Mr Hot Head, who caught my eyes staring at him. He may have felt the heat from my gaze. Everyone knew that my wounds from our first encounter, the psychological ones, had not really fully healed.

He remained my 'bête noire'.[180] I learnt from the Proverbs not to be friends with an angry man.

"Allow me to be your Judas of necessity."

Judas of necessity? In earlier talks in the canteen, it was conceded by a majority of my colleagues that the story of Jesus may not have been as dramatic without the betrayal of Judas. Mr Hot Head knew that he was cast in that role.

I nearly lost my life for his lack of control. Definitely, my father did not expect a crushed head to happen. Well in that context, Mr Hot Head provided the authentic experience that reset my life. Recalling my encounter with him brought back my self-esteem and confidence.

The past months steeled me with the stoic acceptance that pain is an inevitable part of life's give and take. The exchanges in the canteen turned out to be small steps from ignorance to doubt and cynicism, then enlightenment. I gained wisdom in return and strength of character. It did not come on a silver platter, but it was not cheap either.

When I was in the hospital, Mr Hot Head vowed to deny himself any luxury as a way of penance for his guilt. His shabby way of grooming to show his fondness for Diogenes earned him a sobriquet as 'barrel philosopher'. Diogenes, who had spent time in a barrel reflecting on his philosophy of cynicism, is better known holding a lighted torch in full

---

[180] Someone or something which is particularly disliked.

morning blaze looking for a righteous man in Athens but finding none.

To his credit, Mr Hot Head never ran away from his guilt. He genuinely extended gestures to atone for his reckless behaviour and I never gave him the comfort of accepting his remorse. Perhaps, it was my own way to lighten the load of my own guilt due to my disrespect of my father by making him carry mine.

*

"What is it?"

I heard a friend calling me. He was just in time to sense my introspection—an inkling that something was bothering me. Understanding non-verbal communication and perceiving physiological cues had developed among us in the canteen.

My friends were extremely delighted that when I met my father again, he did not treat me as a prodigal son, and there had not been any recriminations. Instead, he told me that the footprints on the sand during my difficult time in Manila belonged to him. Also, it was a gesture that I am released from the burden of my guilt.

I remember my father always warned me about my curiosity. But he took a great risk allowing me the space to discover for myself what life meant to me and the reward to live in the open. He knew that practical knowledge will not be acquired at home with mere words. He himself had roamed the countryside with peasants as a young man seeking justice.

"What did you learn that your father was afraid of?"

They were curious. It was a question to themselves as much as mine.

241

"I learnt that faith is not hereditary. A genuine Christian life or other spiritual life is for the good heart to discover."

But I was also thinking of my mother's daring. She did not smother me with maternal love, forgoing the protection of the home as a shell. It was she who pushed me out to the open field and like a seed, I grew with the sunlight of reason nourished by the fertile soil of experience. It was nature repeating itself in my life.

Between my father and my mother, my gratitude was in equipoise after I realised the unity of purpose of the two, undoubtedly sparked by parental love.

"A wise son makes a proud father!" one of the students said, concluding that my father was an astute mentor.

"And a proud mother," I added.

Yet, it puzzled me that he did not promptly intervene as soon as he knew of it because my flight from home was also a flight of thought from his belief, before it reached a point antagonistic to his church's doctrines!

They wanted to understand the dilemma that confronted me, about Felix Manalo and the church he founded, the *Iglesia ni Cristo*.

I told them it was a Judeo-Christian faith.

"Jewish because the church relies heavily on the wise teachers of the Old Testament, like the book of Job and Psalm, the Proverbs, let alone Ecclesiastes, but by believing in the new covenant under the New Testament it is a Christian faith."

"Then there is no difference at all. There are no choices to make," someone observed.

"Felix Manalo's message is unique. He preached that Jesus is not God but claims that Jesus' body is his church, the Iglesia. It is a metaphor backed by scriptural passages that are cut here and there from the New Testament and Old Testament prophecies, then read together to explain his theory!"

I told them that Felix Manalo preached that membership in the '*Iglesia*' is the sole path for salvation and individuals outside the church will go to hell.

It came as a shock to them.

"I did not know that membership in a church is the only key to salvation. I thought it is about doing good deeds. If I join your '*Iglesia*' I can smash the head of another philosopher again?" Mr Hot Head jestingly commented.

Mr Hot Head's going to heaven after smashing many heads exposed what was specious in Felix Manalo's message.

If it is not membership, what is it?

The body of Christ or '*Iglesia*' is a metaphor referring collectively to Jesus' Sermon on the Mount, the gospel, including the golden rule. Taken together, these are called a 'body of laws' about love and charity to each other. Living them, not membership or conversion, is the key to salvation.

In the light that I see, the emphasis is goodness and not membership in any church or being labelled as Christian, Muslim, Buddhist or Hindu.

With that I looked at my friends in the canteen no longer as men destined for hell but holding their salvation through their own deeds. Then I thought that even without an afterlife, their goodness per se would contribute bliss to people, a heaven in this world. Such fairness is preferred over an unjust God.

"It must have been a difficult moral choice for your father," a student who majors in Greek Literature noting the distance from my father's belief, interjected.

We felt a gem of an idea was bursting forth.

"That was the dilemma of Agamemnon[181] in the tragic drama of Aeschylus.[182] To win the war against the Trojans, the gods demanded from Agamemnon a sacrifice by killing his own daughter. Your father's choice is either to let you discover your own truth, which means of course to turn his back to his duty to keep you in his church. I can almost hear your father crying like Agamemnon, 'Which of these is without evils?'"

Barok, another student, shifted the burden to me from my father. He never carried a book except for a small notebook and ballpoint pen which always ran out of ink. He was ribbed for being thrifty with those scant resources.

"Why don't we take a page from the philosophers of the baroque era?"

We all laughed thinking that he was toying with his name. There was nothing irregular in his face which characterised the beauty of Baroque art in the seventeenth century, but his fine features were enhanced by his dark complexion, a distinguishing feature of Ilocanos who lived in the barren and hot region north of Luzon. *'Barok'* in Ilocano is the slang for a boy while *'Balasang'* is the opposite equivalent for female. Ilocano elders use them to exhibit their fondness for a child or grandchild.

He raised his hands to quell the outburst and take him seriously. Then we heard the most exotic words; we had adored him since.

*"Carpe diem!"*[183]

"Seize the day!" someone translated it for us.

---

[181] Greek King in the great Trojan War

[182] One of the best writers of Greek Tragedy.

[183] Latin aphorism, the free translation of which is "enjoy yourself while you have the chance".

A commotion ensued among students who were competing to select their music from the jukebox. A newcomer grabbed the collar of one of our old friends after waiting impatiently for a turn to play his favourite Beatle song. Clearly there were pro-Beatles and pro-Elvis on the opposite sides of the aisles, characteristics of the 1960s.

"That is not what I meant," said Barok referring to the rough newcomer who wanted to seize the moment to play the Beatle's 'Love, Love Me Do'.

"Seize the day because tomorrow you will die." Barok recounted that conquering Roman generals who arrived in Rome amid a welcome parade had always someone beside him who whispers *'memento mori'*, [184] reminding him of his mortality. Then *Barok* looked at me in the face.

"Beautiful things are the gift that we have to appreciate but they do not last," he said.

"The love of a father and the son in return is a beautiful exemplar of why we are human. Then the father is gone and what did you do with your opportunity to make him happy while he was alive? I say seize the moment because tomorrow your father or you are gone."

He left the table because he did not want us to see him, the always vivacious guy, our resident comic, cry. Someone quipped that he may have missed his father, but his close friend disclosed that he never knew his father and we were the brothers he had never had.

"We always laughed with his anecdotes and antics, but did you not notice that he never laughed in return?" Comedians are so-called not because they are funny inside but because we

---

[184] The exact English translation: "Remember, you must die!"

laugh at them. I saw the new '*Barok*': the serious and reflective guy.

It dawned on me that my friends at the canteen had each kept a secret, including Mr Hot Head who left before I could tell him, "That all is well that ends well".

*

My father was in Manila for the preparations leading to the fiftieth-anniversary celebration of the church. He is now more comfortable that his son appears pursuing the right path.

I chose not to tell him that the church no longer offers the ambience to nurture my spiritual fire. Whenever I saw people in worship being moved by the pulpit, I am reminded of Shakespeare's tale that life is

"...a walking shadow, a poor player that struts and frets his hour upon the stage. And then is heard no more... full of sound and fury, signifying nothing."[185]

Manny fetched me the following afternoon to attend a dress rehearsal of a 'tableau' [186] of the fiftieth anniversary of the church at the Araneta Coliseum.[187] He was happy that I did not refuse. After all, my father was a big part of that fifty years and he and his peers had contributed immensely to that growth. That is a treasured memory in the family.

The entire rehearsal depicted the church's fifty years of unprecedented progress from a very humble beginning to a

---

[185] A quote spoken in Macbeth conveying that life is brief and meaningless.

[186] A group of models representing a scene from a story or from history.

[187] An indoor multi-purpose sports arena with a seat capacity of 16,500.

nationwide phenomenon with the new leader, the son Eraño Manalo, casting his eyes on expansion worldwide for the next fifty years.

The establishment of worship centres abroad for church members will meet the church doctrine of faithful attendance on Thursday and Sunday services. My father found himself in the crosshairs of this issue as the emigrating member or an entire family would seek his advice and blessing for their decision to emigrate to where there are no places of worship. He would grant the blessings, invoking God's promise of his presence where two or more meet in his name.

I lit up watching the tableau unfold and the pride in the crowd was unmistakable. But it was not enough to animate me from within. I have gone past the enchantment of religion after learning about persecutions, intimidations, bloodletting, and death all in the name of partisan religious truth or, more correctly, untruth.

I could see fanaticism and violent tendencies in the works from the frenzy of the faithful. The conduct of the church police who saw an enemy in me with the slight hint of apostasy as just the tip of an iceberg. An ugly premonition nags me that soon when this church grows with power and wealth, the preservation of these sinecures will be a cause to persecute or even harm any member or anyone perceived to be a threat.

The persecution of the innocent will now come from within not from outside the sect. Like the execution of St Augustine's 'Just War'[188] and the crusaders' violence to regain

---

[188] Aurelius Augustinus or St Augustine, the patron saint of brewers, held that we do not seek peace to be at war, but we go to war that we may have peace.

247

the holy land, or the unreasonable mayhem of the inquisition, the faithful of this growing church will feel no guilt being blindfolded by faith, as for them the end will justify the means. The unfolding of one of the deadly sins which is a warning from the Proverbs—their 'hands shed innocent blood' repeating itself in this church![189]

I recalled Samuel Taylor Coleridge's warning of such a church:

"He who begins loving Christianity better than the Truth, will proceed by loving his sect or church better than Christianity, and end in loving himself better than all."

The final minutes of the presentation changed my nonchalance. A young lady not yet twenty years old was clad in a Filipina *terno*[190] of red, white and blue, the colours of the Philippine flag, depicting the mother Philippines. Her beauty was as powerful as her rendition of 'Mi Ultimo Adios'[191] the swansong of the Philippines' national hero, Jose Rizal, before his execution. The piece secretly hidden in a lamp was passed as a bequeath to Rizal's sister on the latter's visit on the hero's last night. That fiery poem sustained the fervour of the revolution which ended the three hundred and thirty-three years of Spanish colonisation. Then sixteen years later, in

---

[189] Proverbs 6:16-19 There are six things the Lord hates, seven that are detestable to him: haughty eyes, a lying tongue, hands that shed innocent blood, a heart that devises wicked schemes, feet that are quick to rush into evil, a false witness who pours out lies, and a person who stirs up conflict in a community.

[190] A gown with butterfly sleeves.

[191] A poem written by the country's national hero kept secretly in his jail lamp. There is a big religious issue of his "retraction" of his tirade against the church.

1914, the fulfillment of the prophecy on the emergence of the last messenger of God in the Far East with the founding of the *Iglesia ni Cristo.*

A feeling stirred inside me which made my heart sing at the conclusion of the poem by the lady symbolising the Philippines. Before, when I took the bus from Santiago, the stirring within me was the curiosity of the unknown, now there was an unexplained feeling that moved me, like I have reached the highest point of my journey. Looking and hearing her voice brought peace within me and now the world with my father would likewise be peaceful.

Manny told me that the young actress was a student in the university belt who, while in the girls' high school, was elected the student presiding officer of the Manila City Council during the Boys and Girls Week. She was a lithe twelve-year-old when she was tapped to deliver speeches in the presidential campaign of then President Carlos P. Garcia.[192]

The significance of that unique sensation was unlocked after the death of my father thirteen years later. My wife told me that my father called her to have a private talk about me. He said that he was happy and comforted about my choice of a wife and that assured him of my faith about remaining in the church. He told her about my never-ending questions about nature, life, and the doctrine of the church. Many things, he said, cannot be explained with a reason but just what the holy spirit would inspire you into believing.

The confidence and reliance on my wife were not misplaced. After all, she was that last act in the tableau, embracing the arrival and preaching of the message of God by

---

[192] 8th President of the Philippines (1957 – 1961)

his last messenger in the church doctrine, Felix Manalo. A powerful snapshot of the church's fifty years anniversary.

*

There were many summers after that before the inevitable took place. It came unexpectedly in 1981, just after the birth of my third and last child. My father died after nearly fifty years in the ministry.

Upon the pronouncement of his death, my mother embraced me and in muted sobs expressed her fears.

"What will happen to me now?"

We told her that we would take care of her the way she took care of us growing up and even with her grandchildren. "Besides, the church will be there," I said.

I was wrong.

At his wake, we chose a non-expensive casket to lighten the burden on the church when a senior bespectacled minister who personified the pioneering spirit of the old school of ministers, called our attention to the fact that it did not fit the stature of my father in the Ministry. We upgraded it a little bit to comply with that kind-hearted soul but still in keeping with my father's view of death as 'dust to dust'.

A week after the internment, I was called by the church hierarchy and reported with my wife to the national auditor of the church in charge of finances. He showed us the expenses incurred and asked us to reimburse it, including the cost of the casket, which caused me to feel aghast. When we admitted that we did not have the cash for it, he required me to issue unfunded post-dated cheques instead and after doing so, I just left in a huff from the suffocating feeling of disappointment. I did not bother then about how to source the unfunded cheque; I left the guy without even looking at his proud bald-headed face, to me, Socrates' and Tata Abon's antithesis.

My father did not have social security insurance like all the other ministers and those in the employ of the church's support services. They were all classified as volunteers even when the church had grown in membership and wealth, and their activities were actually regular functions of the church.

I recall my father telling me that they were contributing to the 'sundries'[193] deducted from every pay called 'monetary assistance' and this was supposedly their social security insurance to take care of their old age.

But it turned out not to be the case. However sad it was, it was opportune for us children to take care of a parent. The unfair and undeserved inattention by the church leadership was suffered in silence not to tear apart our father's cherished life as minister. So, we played chasse for the church duty for the widow of one of its pioneers.

Five years before her death was belle epoque, [194] when she received a dole from the church. At ninety-eight years old, her senility barely realised the injustice from the church nor the belated enlightenment of the church elders.

Perhaps, it was serendipity that many years later, I was appointed as the Chairman of the Social Security Commission of the Philippines.

The appointment gave me the opportunity to urge all church organisations in the Philippines to register their workers in the Social Security System. This policy did not

---

[193] Amount set aside for a future need.

[194] Literally means 'Beautiful Age' referring to an era of peace and plenty.

please the church hierarchy and other religious groups when they realised billions of past dues of contributions and penalties for the social security of unregistered ministerial and support services workers.

It was ironic that the factual reality of those whose commitment and labour was to save souls was smacked of hypocrisy and insincerity by disregarding the future security of their workers. I was an inconvenient reminder of their failings and only my removal from the social security system would ease the torment of their conscience.

In contrast, the first to comply was the Bishop of Cubao, [195] of the Roman Catholic Church who received a commendation from the Social Security System for its initiative. It was his personal choice to do what is right and what is good for his religious workers.

\*

My children would ask me what their grandfather was like. I told them about my father playing chess or ping-pong with his children and they were athirst by the paucity of my reminiscence.

They learnt more about the meaning of my father's legacy in the 'Valdez Open', a family affair I organised in his honour and memory every December.

Here is a scene in one of the competitions which was reported in my tabloid column:

*"It was the third rack of the best of the three billiard eight-*

---

[195] Commercial centre of Quezon City, the most populous city in the Philippines.

*ball championship round in the 2003 Valdez Open. The event is one of the highlights of my family's welcome treat to the New Year for the past two years.*

*Both players in the championship round have cleaned up their respective solid and striped coloured balls. It was my turn, the father, to hit the white ball with the eight ball at the brink of the left-side pocket. All I have to do is to sink the eight ball to win the championship and the P500 first prize from the tight wallet of the house treasurer, my wife.*

*Earlier I eliminated Jojo, my second son who is now an architect. In an 'Efren Bata' fashion my youngest son, Jason (now a medical doctor), eliminated the eldest, Melquiades, my father's namesake (now a lawyer) to arrange the title showdown with me. Actually, the youngest is the defending champion having won the crown in the first Valdez Open the previous year.*

*What I was going to do would perhaps shatter Jason's desire to retain his crown. If I will intentionally miss the ball and make him win, it would have been a supreme sacrifice for a father to make his son happy. But if the son gets the crown and the five hundred in that manner I would unwittingly destroy the values of honesty and fairness.*

*In that brief moment before hitting the cue ball, I thought of the choices parents made involving their children... So I hit the cue ball with the intention of putting the winning ball in the pocket. And... I missed the championship... but left a genuine legacy to my sons. That is the best prize!"*

It was the ultimate test.

Then I realised... my father had been smiling at me all along in my journey. I smiled to him in return!

# 15
# CONSEQUENCES

My first two years in Manila since I arrived there one afternoon with a pair of old shoes and hand-me-down pants and shirts were interesting and exciting times indeed. Feat after feat, doses of loss, learning to overcome my fears, and many challenges pushed me further from my parents' long shadows.

The passing of time went on unnoticed but productive and memorable in terms of my real and practical education. It prepared me to play a role, no matter how insignificant, in the future political events in the country.

Emily Dickenson, the eminent writer who coincidentally shares the same birthdate as my father, captured the thoughts that emboldened and guided me:

"I dwell in Possibility... More numerous windows, Superior of doors... The spreading wide of narrow hands to gather Paradise."

My peers at the canteen contributed to the way I saw things. I could feel the wind fresher and freer to engage in new battles, but the counsel of that multitude of young men was a restraint against being reckless and foolish.

*

It was the start of the decade of the '60s. We shared the euphoria of John F. Kennedy's election as President of the United States but his brinkmanship in the Cuban Missile Crisis heightened our sense of insecurity with the presence of the US military bases in the Philippines.

We reacted with collective relief that the fingers of doom did not pull the trigger of the nuclear guns. We realised the built-in deterrence to go to war with the fear of mutual annihilation of either the US or the USSR. Still, we debated on which side to take, and we were unanimous in choosing the high moral ground on the side of the West as the Berlin Wall reminded us of the lack of freedom in the socialist and communist states.

After the Cuban Missile Crisis, Mao Tse Tung in 1962 embarked his own cultural revolution that made the Chinese realise that it was not enough to change government for a country to succeed but that a change of thinking was necessary as well. It was planned as a re-education of the people to arrest the slide to a capitalist society where its ugly face shows a privilege defined by the wealth of the few at the expense of the many. Instead, power changed hands from one group to the other while Mao Tse Tung watched from his perch. It was a bloody struggle where the pendulum swung from one group to the other, particularly the youth. Foreign intervention did not rear its ugly head which was fortuitous for the Chinese because this internal experiment was the fine-tuning of the Chinese collective mind as well as statecraft that decided policy direction on the basis of the Chinese interest and model. China in the more than a decade of soul-searching, and internecine struggle, teetered on the verge of collapse but Mao's charisma and venerable repute held and many years later after his death, the sleeping dragon woke to its full potential.

As events unfurled, the Camelot in Kennedy's court was obliterated by a single assassin's bullet in 1963 but not before Kennedy gave impetus to the Vietnam War which reached the height of mayhem at the time I served as a lawyer of the Seventh Fleet in the US Naval Base in Subic Bay in the early '70s. The gore of that military misadventure produced the most cruel and heartless human armed contingent with the massacre of about four hundred civilians in a South Vietnamese village of My Lai on March 16, 1968, by American soldiers. But outside My Lai, there were losers, one of which was our sense of empathy because we were not vocal enough to protest the atrocity committed to our brother Asians.

The highest irony to be told in the aftermath of My Lai was to erase what Kennedy had earned in life as a man of peace. Instead, his hubris as an alpha male in paving the way to the Vietnam War made him the fool of a man years after his death. The souls of those killed in that crazy Vietnam War became the curse to the United States to gradually lose its moral predominance and a burden to the national conscience.

This new war had tremendous implications to the way of life and political narrative of the Filipinos. To the more ideologically minded among our friends in the canteen, the Americans were committing double-speak by the perceived intervention of the CIA in the presidential elections in 1965. The scent of Kennedy's triumph in the Cuban Missile Crisis made America smell bad to the Filipino nationalists. They were still seen as engaged in the puppetry of our leaders.

It was recalled that when the US finally give the Filipino political independence in 1946, there was no Marshall Plan like the programme that rebuilt Europe after the war. Instead, they kept control of the resources needed to build an economically self-reliant state by having total control of the country's economic apparatus. They simply bullied their way by taking advantage of the ruins of the just-concluded war by installing Manuel Roxas as president in cahoots with the Filipino sugar barons and political powerbrokers, and by enshrining a provision in the Philippine constitution a parity clause, a euphemism for total control. It was painful and indelicate because they ousted the elected representatives of the peasants who opposed the parity provision.

Clearly, America was destroying the democratic institution it had built, including the free market that goes with it to ensure its success. Again, human greed reared its head with imperialist designs disguised as Manifest Destiny to impart statecraft in the Philippines.

By that misleading word 'parity', [196] the country's economy, then better than most of Asia including Japan, would go downhill mainly because the country was not economically independent. Better still, the entire country was blinded by a sense of security being economically attached to the American apron and its territorial defence put entirely under the US military umbrella.

*

Towards the middle of 1964, the political pot was boiling. Then, Senate President Ferdinand Marcos, in a masterful

---

[196] Granting US citizens and corporations rights to Philippine natural resources equal to those of Philippine citizens.

move, bolted from the ruling Liberal Party of President Macapagal and captured the nomination of the rival Nacionalista Party, [197] as the latter's standard-bearer. This paved the way for him to be elected overwhelmingly as president of the country under the slogan, "This nation can be great again."

In one of our talks in the canteen, the young students were talking about Marcos having been convicted of murder for the death of the political adversary of his father and while in jail he reviewed for the bar examinations, the toughest government exams in the country and topped it. Afterwards, on appeal of his conviction, he argued to the Supreme Court for his acquittal. It was a stuff that makes a living legend of Marcos who, instead of being rejected by the electorate because of that taint of blood in his hands, was hailed as a hero.

One of the perceptive students in our midst commented that Marcos did not just leave his desires to the whims of pure fate but seized them. Marcos' feat ennobled us and collectively we were moved to act as well.

'*Carpe Diem*' became the spirit of our generation!

Actually, Marcos was just following the precedent of another charismatic personality, the then Congressman Ramon Magsaysay [198] in 1954 who himself was a member of the Liberal Party but joined the Nacionalista Party as presidential candidate and won as president with the assistance of the Americans.

Ironically, the same man was behind this repeat of history

---

[197] The oldest political party in the Philippines.
[198] 7th President of the Philippines (1953 – 1957)

in the person of Jose P. Laurel[199] who was the country's president in World War II under the auspices of the Japanese occupation forces. The accounts show that old Laurel, who as a member of the country's Supreme Court before World War II, was bewitched by Ferdinand Marcos, but not before he had doubts that Ferdinand Marcos topped the bar after reviewing for the examinations while in jail. The members of the high court thought that in ordinary experience, Marcos could not have concentrated well enough to emerge as number one in the bar examinations. For this, the Supreme Court again subjected Marcos to an oral inquiry and the result impressed the magistrates even more, especially Laurel, who found in the young man qualities of leadership. Laurel, the influential leader of the Nacionalista Party, played a role in making Marcos the party's presidential standard-bearer against the very popular incumbent president, Diosdado Macapagal, of the ruling Liberal Party.

Ramon Magsaysay was also plucked from the Liberal Party in 1953 through Laurel as the Nacionalista Party's standard-bearer for president against President Elpidio Quirino.[200] Magsaysay also won overwhelmingly and was hailed as 'Man of the Masses'—an accolade lovingly bestowed. He died in a plane crash out of Cebu City on a March 1957 night as the presidential plane had just taken off on a return flight to Manila.

*

---

[199] President of the Philippines during the Japanese occupation.
[200] 6th President of the Philippines (1948 – 1953).

In 1967, Ramon Magsaysay, Jr, the son of the late president, was elected to his father's old congressional district of Zambales where I served in his congressional staff. I was privileged to do chores for this son of a legendary president, preparing letters, memoranda and drafting bills and sometimes being assigned to write simple speeches on minor occasions.

But on important policy matters, the speeches were written mostly by a young political activist and debater who had graduated at the University of the Philippines College of Law. Heherson 'Sonny' Alvarez also hailed from Santiago, Isabela where he showed at an early age the promise of being a national leader and ideological pacesetter on the left of the political spectrum.

We shared the urgent need to correct the disproportionate economic and social structure. To do this, there must be a change of the peoples' understanding of their rights and responsibilities to themselves and the community. This common aspiration connected us to a friendship that lasted until he died in 2020 of infection from the lethal coronavirus.

He later became one of the most articulate critics of President Marcos and went on exile in the United States when martial law was declared in 1972.

About two decades later, in 1986, he became a Minister of Agrarian Reform and, being out of touch for a long time from the Philippine milieu after a forced exile to the United States, he requested me to advise him on legal matters, putting me at the helm of the Department's Bureau of Agrarian Legal Assistance where we established the very effective 'Barefoot Lawyers Program' that resulted in the resolution of at least 5,000 old agrarian cases. One of these cases included the fifty-year-old 'Jalajala-Meralco case' involving small farmers and the behemoth power distribution company in the country.

In the Ministry of Agrarian Reform, Sonny and I went around the country to speak with farmers who were at first hostile to our peace offensive and at one instance would even put roadblocks on the runway to prevent our small plane from landing so that we would be forced to land in another city in Panay Island.[201]

It was not only the people for or against the proposed agrarian reform programme of President Cory Aquino who showed hostility but at one instance the weather was inhospitable. On the way from Tuguegarao to Manila, on board a ten-seater plane with some members of media, we encountered zero visibility for a good ten minutes. In one or two instances, the air pocket would jolt the plane for at least ten metres down, our breath held bated as the pilot flew the small plane relying solely on the radar instruments.

Another experience was quite comical when I was asked to bring a sacrificial dog on a helicopter ride from Manila to the mountain lair of Commander Balweg, a priest who turned rebel and the head of a big communist band in the Cordilleras which is in the northern Philippines. The dog was to be butchered as offering in a native ritual to be performed after a truce for peace is signed. I was relieved that Sonny's dog was spared because the natives had their own to use in that event. Since then whenever I visited Sonny at his home, his dog, the sacrificial lamb so to speak, would welcome me with his tail wagging in excitement as though he knew how his life was

---

[201] 6th largest and 4th most populous island in the Philippines. The famous white sand powdery beach of Boracay Island is located in its northwest province of Aklan.

spared.

This gave me the opportunity to get in touch with the tenants and small landowners all over the country, including the former *hukbalahap* founder and 'Supremo'[202] Luis Taruc. He had been a fierce resistance leader during World War II against the Japanese occupation forces and one of those who was ousted as an elected leader in the House of Representatives after the war because of his stand against the parity rights for American citizens. I gained invaluable insights from them on how to improve their lot and learnt how to address the agrarian problem.

In one instance in 1987, Sonny and I were invited to visit and observe the farmers in action in Japan and one late evening, we were fetched from our hotel in Tokyo by a farmer with a brand new Pajero[203] that brought us to the outskirts of the city. It was already sunset when we reached the farm and in the midst of darkness in the open field, I heard chirping sounds like a weird welcome. To allay my apprehension, our host told me that those were sounds of silkworms eating leaves of mulberry trees. He pointed to me the many huts dotting the landscape where the worms are housed and within the radius of many kilometres the farmer's cooperative produced silk that they supplied to the textile mills. He said that silk production has improved the productivity of the farmers who have additional income besides the cultivation of the soil.

It occurred to me that agriculture and industrial production when in tandem, each feeding the other, are a potent force to the nation's overall economic output if they are

---

[202] A person of highest rank in power and authority.
[203] Mid-sized sport utility vehicle.

harnessed together. Even then, I concluded that it was more important to address the farmers' productivity than the very idealistic and controversial confiscation of land and awarding it to the farmers.

The cloak-and-dagger sort of talks with the underground communists who wanted to be heard regarding their agrarian grievances prepared Sonny Alvarez to draft a Comprehensive Agrarian Reform Program when the former was elected Senator of the Philippines. The sometimes secretive and informal colloquy with the underground peasants as well as the public and formal dialogue with the officers of their front organisations gave me a better understanding of their plight, which helped me contribute to Alvarez's efforts to write the historic law.

When I became the National Director of the Integrated Bar of the Philippines' Legal Aid Program, I designed a programme that addressed the concerns of those sons and daughters of farmers who migrated to the urban centres and who, because of hardships, got entangled in legal problems that required free legal aid services.

The total immersion and exchanges with them and with experts on different issues on economics, society, industrialisation, agricultural production, infrastructure development, domestic and foreign trade, policy planning and implementation and a variety of related fields had prepared me to engage in public discussions on current issues in the different national media platforms and in the TV/radio programme, *Magpayo nga Kayo*, [204] which I hosted in the largest TV network in the Philippines for a little more than a

---

[204] Literally translated "Please give your advice".

dozen years. It was billed as an informal school of common sense which was formatted as one of 'brainstorming on the air' with the people from all walks of life. Even the rebels in the mountain would call to air their views while government officials would listen as well to develop ideas that could address in a practical manner many of the daily problems that affected the general public.

*

In the later part of 2000, at about six o'clock in the evening, I received a call from Sonny Alvarez who asked me if I had watched the privilege speech of one of the senators at the Senate of Philippines, Teofisto Guingona, exposing the then incumbent President Joseph 'Erap' Estrada of Corruption and Betrayal of Public Trust. Sonny was then a representative of Isabela to the House of Congress of the Philippines, the equivalent of the House of Commons in the United Kingdom and the House of Representatives of the United States.

When I said yes, he asked me to draft a Complaint of Impeachment which he filed with the House of Representative Committee on Justice the following day.

After committee hearings, an 'Article of Impeachment' was passed by the House of Representatives. The referral to the Senate for trial was attended by treachery, a touch of Machiavelli and Shakespeare to open a historic drama unique in Philippine politics.

It may have been a desperation that called the necessity of such an action. At that point, the two-thirds votes needed to pass the resolution of impeachment hung in the balance as Erap had a majority of the representatives on his side although a good number was sitting on the fence feeling the political winds. So much is said about Dante's hottest seat in hell for those who are neutral, which turned out not for them but for Erap whose greatest hell is yet to come.

At the start of the plenary session, the then Speaker of the House of Representatives, Manuel Villar, who was Erap's handpicked choice for the House's helm, started with a ruse. The calm belied the storm to come. He led the unsuspecting plenary with a prayer and then his voice went into a crescendo, dropping the pious tone into a wordplay, becoming the sponsorship speech to transmit the 'Article of Impeachment' to the Senate for trial. A stunned audience forgot to speak, or perhaps some muted any objection, and when they finally realised the legal end, the motion of impeachment and transmittal to the Senate was carried with the two-thirds majority required under the constitution. The fence sitters now joined the clamour of the winning partisans to legitimise a deceit into a 'fait accompli'.[205]

The trial of the impeached popular president, the man who called himself *'Erap para sa Mahihirap'*[206] ground the nation practically to a standstill on all economic, political and social fronts. Yet, despite the allegations, he held on to his unprecedented popularity and there is no doubt that he was endeared in the hearts of the great masses of Filipino people. Either they did not believe that he was guilty or they decided they can close their eyes to give him a second chance.

In survey after survey, his approval ratings did not suffer

---

[205] A thing that has already happened before those affected hear about it, leaving them no option but to accept it.
[206] Erap for the poor!

a dent and all fingers point to his acquittal. Philippine politics at that moment was a bittersweet romance between its leader and the governed; a test for the latter.

At that time, I was Dean of a Law School which was owned by a taipan[207] who was known to have supported Estrada financially when he ran for president. To the credit of the administration of the school, they did not object to my being one of the private prosecutors in the trial and I would have resigned my post as dean had they required me to choose between my work and being part of history. But the school administration remained faithful to truth and constitutional processes which is what an institution of learning should do.

Then there was an issue during the trial of Erap at the Senate that changed the course of events. It was the opening of an envelope that was submitted by one of Erap's depository banks which supposedly contained the smoking gun, the savings or current accounts of Erap's money imagined to be in billions of pesos. Erap's defence team did not want it to be opened and presented technical grounds to oppose the opening.

When the issue was presented to a vote, after a gestation of emotion rose to a pent-up level, the 'NO' votes prevailed.

The streets came alive with demonstrations of people for and against Erap. Then the public and private prosecutors decided to walk out of the impeachment trial in full view of the whole nation who were glued to their TV sets watching a 'cause celebre'[208] feeding the frenzy of the masses to such kind of real-time drama.

---

[207] Powerful billionaire businessman of Chinese descent.
[208] Celebrated case.

Erap's grip on his government broke loose.

Eventually, Erap's ouster was dictated by the multitude in EDSA, [209] a main thoroughfare far from the seat of power, composed of a mix of the elite and the middle class, but considered miniscule compared to the 'hoi polloi'[210] that made the bulk of his support.

Abraham Lincoln had said that "God must love the common man, he made so many of them." If he were to judge this tumultuous populace, he would not have hesitated to vouch for Erap because of their number, and then the outcome would have been different.

Martin Luther, a great religious reformer, had referred to them as "the murdering and thieving rabble of the peasants." But times had changed because in the sideshow among the religious groups composed mostly of the common people, the leader of the pro-ouster group was the Catholic cardinal who also sought the ouster of Marcos a decade and a half ago, while the opposite number in support of Erap is the executive minister of the *Iglesia ni Cristo* which has already grown into a force to be reckoned with in Philippine politics.

Reminiscing about the event, Erap confided in me. He told me that during his discussion with his defence lawyers he had wanted the envelope to be opened but his chief defence counsel had prevailed against it on technical grounds. It was shown later that the account did not contain any amount. The gut feeling of the unschooled Erap, the main strength of his character, gave way to the logic of the professionals who were

---

[209] Main highway in Metro Manila covering five big cities named Epifanio De Los Santos Avenue.

[210] Masses, common people.

experts in law but deaf to the people's pulse.

\*

After Erap's release from prison, he showed no rancour or bitterness to all those who had conspired to oust him and those who participated in the legal process by virtue of their expertise in the law. He is not above being emotional, however, because as related to me by Ombudsman Aniano Desierto in Erap's arraignment at the Sandiganbayan or the graft court, when he was called to approach the justices for his plea, he stopped at 'Ani' Desierto, the chief prosecutor, and told him in his thespian voice, "You are too cruel", an understandable outburst from a former president who finds himself in the lowest depth of his life. To my knowledge, that was the extent of his bitterness to those who had done him wrong.

No one could have told him to his face not to cry like a woman for the downfall of the kingdom he failed to defend. While he did not have a castle any more, he presided every Sunday over a roundtable lunch at his famous Polk Street residence in North Greenhills where the multi-awarded actor had still enough fiction and charisma to recreate success and failure. This was a platform for his jokes with his regular guests, his friends from different walks and discipline, which belied from the outside that he was nursing a psychological wound inside.

As I was one of the regulars on the luncheon roundtable for years, I saw him up close and personal. He may have his faults and many loves, but he was a sincere human being, loyal to a fault to a friend and was always happy to offer his help generously to those in need. His slogan, *'Erap Para sa*

*Mahihirap*' was not an empty cry in battle but natural to him. Starting as a teen or even younger when he would empty the family cupboard to share food with starving neighbours even while his family was large and not financially endowed for this kind of philanthropy.

It may have been a balm to him that in succeeding years in the launching of the book on the life of Speaker Jose de Venecia, Jr his adversary in the 1998 presidential election, former President Cory Aquino, [211] the icon of the first 'Edsa Revolution'[212] apologised to him for the impeachment that had led to his unjust ouster from the Presidency.

It was not long before he was again nearly elected to the Presidency, but in succeeding elections he was elected to another public office as the Mayor of the City of Manila, an elective position second only in importance and significance to being the president of the country.

*Ostinato rigore* for power? Or destiny's way to give him a second chance?

\*

The succession of Gloria Macapagal-Arroyo to the Presidency was sort of a coming home to Malacañang where she resided as the young daughter of then-President Diosdado Macapagal. She could have been elected to succeed Erap legally after the latter's term of six years, but the peaceful revolution had intervened. Four years later, she was elected President under

---

[211] 11<sup>th</sup> President of the Philippines (1986 – 1992).
[212] Peaceful people power revolution that led to the ouster of sitting President Marcos.

her own terms beating Erap's best friend and hugely popular movie star, Fernando Poe Jr. On this election of Gloria, the original men who had helped her become president and had served in her first administration — with me among them as her Chief Government Corporate Counsel [213] — were no longer in the government.

The victory of Gloria over Fernando or Ronnie Poe was not a decent one million plurality because of the perceived manipulation of the ballots in Mindanao, the southern part of the country rich with Muslim voters. A big controversy came about from a telephone conversation between Gloria and one of the Commission on Election commissioners who was in charge of the Muslim region. Called the 'Garci tapes', the evidence was so incriminatory that it compelled Gloria to say "I am sorry" on prime-time television after most of her cabinet members had resigned from their posts and her administration was teetering to the brink.

Either the appetite for demonstrations in the streets for her ouster had waned or her pardon of Erap had quieted a sizeable portion of the populace that kept her in the Presidency.

As president, she initiated various economic and tax laws which were hard to swallow but then these were the bitter pills that led to the recovery of the economy.

Filipinos would still realise that for every such hard and unpopular choice of a leader the results are lasting benefits to the nation. Gloria's tax laws had steeled the country to be strong and resilient to withstand the effects of regional and international financial crises. Other countries speak of their own sacrifices as key to national unity and pride, like the

---

[213] Chief Legal Counsel of all Government Corporations.

Russians burning Moscow to save Russia from the occupation of Germans and Napoleonic forces, or the Russian peasants butchering millions of cattle to show their disagreement with the ruling communists' forced implementation of the collectives. The Filipinos have yet to make such kind of conscious sacrifice.

Like Erap before her, Gloria was also charged with plunder and was on hospital arrest for the entire term of six years of her successor even as she was elected as representative of the old congressional district of her father in the province of Pampanga. She was succeeded by the son of President Corazon 'Cory' Aquino who had succeeded Marcos, years earlier.

*

Benigno Aquino III or Noynoy was at the right place at the right time when before the nomination of candidates for president his mother, Cory, died. Her death generated a strong public outpouring of condolences and people lined the streets at her funeral.

Filipinos always speak well of the dead and to speak ill of the qualification of Noynoy would have been speaking ill of Cory. That deafening silence about Noynoy's unfitness made another Aquino a president for six years, which encouraged political pundits to quip that death is the prelude to any Aquino presidency. But then, it was also death at the last years of Noynoy's presidency, the botched Mamasapano massacre, [214]

---

[214] The massacre of 44 Philippines Police Commandos in Mamasapano, Maguindanao by terrorists.

that would possibly erase the chances of another Aquino ever becoming a president again.

\*

In the midterm elections of Noynoy's term, Grace Poe, Fernando Poe's daughter, was elected a Senator, a position good enough for her to be in the public eye, and the kingmakers made her a viable candidate for president in the election of 2016.

The year preceding the May 2016 presidential elections looked unexciting because there was only one who stood to be unchallenged and invincible as successor.

He was the hardworking Vice President Jejomar 'Jojo' Binay who had been a long-time mayor of the City of Makati, the financial centre of the country. He declared early for the presidency putting himself under microscopic scrutiny.

At first glance, it was not a miscalculation. He had been a close ally of Noynoy's mother, Cory, and for his self-appointed role as her rabid defender at the earlier years of her Presidency in the 1980s where coup after coup attempts were made by disgruntled military men who were politicised during the later years of the Marcos regime through a secretive group called the Reform the Armed Forces Movement or RAM. He earned the sobriquet 'Rambo' after he was caught on TV and in newspaper headlines showing him armed to the teeth with a submachine gun while manning the roads leading to the Malacañang Palace.[215]

---

[215] Official residence and principal workplace of the President of the Philippines.

He was not a Johnny-come-lately to President Cory, as before that, he had been a human rights lawyer defending the cause of left-orientated groups and even the rebels and Marcos oppositionists. In one of his advocacies, I was in the same court with him in the capital of Zambales, Iba, months before the death by assassination of Cory's husband, Ninoy Aquino, a former senator, whose death had galvanised the people to mount a strong opposition to Marcos' stronghold on government. Binay was defending some people who were accused of having rebelled against the government while I was there doing my own legal work. He was unpretentious and very ordinary looking during our encounter and I was even amused that after the hearing outside the courtroom while exchanging pleasantries, he took off his white cotton *'Barong Tagalog'*, a formal court dress code, put on a T-shirt and just folded his papers to take the first public bus going back to a four-hour bus ride to Manila.

I did not even realise then that he would soon become a mayor of the richest city of the Philippines and many years hence, we became friends and *'compadres'*.[216]

*

For the incumbent President Noynoy, Binay's past services were forgotten. The administration Liberal Party made a systematic demolition job looking into all his projects in Makati City with audit reports of overpricing and anomalies in the bidding process. It was not surprising that people had suspected a conspiracy to promote the candidacy of the

---

[216] Wedding sponsor to one's child.

potential Liberal Party official candidate, Mar Roxas, the grandson of the first President of the Philippine Republic and a scion of multi-billion real estate infrastructure in the centre of Metro Manila. Mar Roxas and Noynoy Aquino belong to the family of elite while Binay was of a lower caste notwithstanding his loyalty to former President Cory Aquino.

But Mar did not sit well with the peoples' liking; they found him to lack a genuine identity with them especially that he anchored his campaign on being 'Mr Palengke'[217] visiting marketplaces which were not in sync with his branded, designer rubber shoes. He had a good track record owing to the fact that he had been a Secretary of Trade, then a Secretary of Transportation and the incumbent Secretary of Local Government. But the people mistook his hesitancy in making decisions as a sign of weakness in character and lack of leadership qualities. He was perceived to be apathetic which he reinforced by what was thought as refusing to send aid to the victims of typhoon 'Yolanda', which caused untold suffering to the people of the provinces of Leyte and Samar, a known political bailiwick of the Marcoses. His wife, a talented and multi-awarded TV and radio host of ABS-CBN, the country's premier media network, aggravated the situation in her widely reported hot and bitter exchange with Anderson Cooper, an anchor and correspondent of CNN, the broad-based and international media network, where she defended what she perceived to be a negative reporting that reflected on her husband on the part of the American news correspondent.

Roxas' closeness with President Noynoy in fact was his political albatross after the mishandling of the military's

---

[217] Meaning "Mr Market Guy" to identify with the lowly.

Mamasapano[218] incident that resulted in the deadly ambush by a renegade group of Muslim separatists which left in its aftermath 44 corpses of Special Action Forces, an elite group of the Philippine National Police. A visit to the remains of the policemen who were laid in an air force military camp was even skipped by President Noynoy in favour of the ribbon cutting in a nearby Japanese car facility event.

Immediately, with the two candidates' campaign in tatters, the civil society, a disparate but potent group consisting of the religious, civic and professionals who spearheaded the downfall of Marcos and Erap, had a new champion in Grace Poe.

*

Grace Poe was perceived to have the command of the votes that rallied behind her father Fernando, Jr. when he ran unsuccessfully for president against Gloria Macapagal Arroyo. But she had an Achilles heel that caught my eye and my action afterwards helped changed the direction of the presidential winds.

Grace Poe had materialised from nowhere. She was adopted by the couple, Fernando Poe, Jr. and his wife, Susan Roces, reputedly the 'King and Queen' of Philippine movies. There is a persistent rumour that she was the daughter of former President, Ferdinand Marcos. There are those who claim this as true because of the likeness of Grace to the

---

[218] 5th class municipality in Maguindanao province in southern Philippines which was the site of an encounter between Philippine military and Muslim rebels.

mother of the late strongman. There are even pictures which if electronically superimposed would make that likeness so close. But all these were denied and could just be a pastime spiel especially in a rumour mill covering showbiz and politics.

She was first appointed by President Noynoy Aquino as head of the MTRCB, the acronym of the Movie and Television Review and Classification Board. She made this her platform to be in the public eye to be successfully elected in 2013 as Senator of the Philippines. During this time, Ferdinand's son, Ferdinand Jr., or 'Bongbong' to his friends was her colleague. Some would allege that they heard him call her 'sis' perhaps to exaggerate the rumour and render it unbelievable.

From her Senate seat, many urged her to run for President of the Philippines for the election of 2016. There was a deluge of support from financial and social groups and almost instantly she became a viable presidential candidate.

At about the same time, I was a frequent and regular Sunday lunch guest of former President Erap Estrada in his private residence. Estrada was a bosom friend of Grace's adoptive father and her baptism godfather. The two popularised the term *'erap'*, an inverted word from *'pare'*, a derivative of *'compadre'* or *'kumpare'* meaning co-parent or brother. During these occasions, the political currents were part of the conversation piece at the main lunch table led by Erap, which included veteran politicians, prominent lawyers, and businessmen. Erap would comment that Grace has the potential for the future but being young and new in politics, 2016 was not yet her time.

I made mention of a possible legal impediment in her candidacy because years before, she renounced her Filipino citizenship when she was naturalised as an American citizen. However, when she was appointed the head of the country's MTRCB, she claimed to have reacquired her Filipino citizenship under a repatriation law. But to be an eligible candidate for president, one must be a natural-born citizen and she lost her original status as such by her renunciation.

Then, Francisco Tatad, a former Senator and former Secretary of Information of the late President Marcos filed a disqualification against Grace Poe alleging that she is not a natural-born citizen mainly because she was a foundling. Another disqualification case was filed by a prominent lawyer who alleged that in addition, she did not have the necessary residency yet to qualify her for the highest elective post. These cases underscored the foundling status of Grace Poe and in a country that had a fetish for the underdog, it boosted her candidacy. The Aquino administration was aware of the unlikely victory of Manuel Roxas and was rumoured to be shifting its support for Grace Poe and this was a big shot in the arm for her candidacy.

*

The political fortunes were shifting among Poe, Binay, and Roxas with the first gaining momentum while the second was on the downturn. Roxas remained to be unexciting and out of the voters' preferred candidates. Many political pundits had cancelled Roxas' chances of a win. Meanwhile, another name was being mentioned: that of the unorthodox Mayor of Davao City, [219] Rodrigo Roa Duterte. He had been in the news for

---

[219] Biggest city in the Philippines based on land area.

many years because of his iron-hand style of leadership. Davao is a southern city that was beset by insurgency, adjoining the secessionist Muslim movement in the autonomous region of Muslim Mindanao and a melting pot with the commonplace problem of peace and order in a thriving and populated metropolis. It is also the biggest city in land area in the Philippines.

The taming of Davao City was Rodrigo Roa Duterte's *la rampe de lancement.* [220] It became the cleanest and most peaceful city in the Philippines—a turnaround from the most violent one just in the recent past. It had helped that Duterte is a lawyer and was a Davao City government prosecutor. He is the son of the former Governor of the province of Davao before it was divided into many Davao provinces later.

During my previous visits in the city a year before the presidential elections, I was amazed by the security and safety of people moving about even in the wee hours of the night. I personally saw a woman jogging at dawn on my way back to the hotel after a meeting with Mayor Duterte and his lawyer friend, Salvador Panelo, now a cabinet-ranked Spokesperson and Chief Presidential Legal Counsel.

My association with Mayor Duterte and Salvador Panelo, who was a member of my law faculty, was remotely connected with the action I took later although Panelo was bruiting about to me five years earlier his pitch on Duterte, egging him to run for the Presidency which the latter declined as he did not have the national constituency. But Panelo was an insistent advocate of an authoritarian model to address the country's problem of discipline, drugs, and graft and corruption in the government

---

[220] Launch pad.

and Duterte fit the bill. Panelo did not realise then that there were quarters who were eyeing a viable run for Duterte, but it was not yet a national and unified move. At the deadline of the filing of the certificate of candidacy for president, Panelo invited me to be at the Manila Hotel to be on hand for Duterte's arrival in Manila from Davao City. There were many expectant supporters and observers at the hotel who were disappointed at Duterte's snub. While unintended, it was reverse psychology at work because it fuelled, even more, the clamour of the handful supporters to push a reluctant candidate to join the presidential run.

In one of the informal discussions of the Philippine Association of Law Schools whose members are all Law Deans in the country, where I served as two-time President and former Chairman of the Board of Trustees, the qualification of Grace Poe for the country's presidency was a hot topic and almost everybody cast doubt on her eligibility. But the Association preferred to maintain a non-political stance since the members represent the public and private law colleges. It fell on me to take up the cudgels.

It was a great dilemma of whether to file or not to file another disqualification case. Besides, my friendship with former President Estrada was in jeopardy. ABS-CBN, where I anchor the long-running radio-TV talk show was not warm on my filing the disqualification case. The network's request not to proceed with the disqualification case, was laced with the hint of command, but doing what they were asking was against the grain of what any self-respecting lawyer would do in that situation. I thought then that the polite overture to dissuade me compromised the network's non-partisan policy. I gave them a graceful exit by announcing in my national programme of a

279

disclaimer about any participation in my filing of the disqualification case.

However, the conduct of the network was not lost to political observers and a few years later, the House of Representatives rejected its bid for the renewal of its franchise on the grounds, among others, of perceived partisanship in every electoral exercise.

*

I filed the disqualification case.

At the time of filing, the momentum of political winds was swinging in favour of Grace Poe, gradually pushing out the frontrunner Jejomar Binay who was increasingly demonised with allegations of graft and corruption during his unchallenged stint as the Mayor of Makati City. Mar Roxas, the chosen candidate of the then incumbent President Noynoy Aquino, has not shown any surge in the polls.

But all that political maths would change. The people started to have a second look at Grace Poe. She was now seen on her own merit and not the borrowed charisma of her adoptive father, the movie king Fernando Poe, Jr. Now, the people saw her as one who had abandoned her country of birth and sought the comfort of life in the United States of America. Her oath of allegiance to the country of her choice abjured any allegiance to the Philippines. To the people, this kind of renunciation categorically turned her back and soul against them. She was no longer a genuine choice for the Presidency.

But the legal battle in the Supreme Court had the earmarks of an extension of the political battle outside. A case that puts in issue the qualification of a presidential candidate must be given priority in the court. But it was not so with the incumbent Chief Justice. She showed a lack of urgency and even wasted precious time just reading the hundreds of positions to be filled up by natural-born Filipinos only. There was a good percentage of voters who were waiting for the decision on the qualification of Grace Poe that would uphold her eligibility. Pundits speculated that a favourable decision would clinch the Presidency for Poe.

Looming over the horizon, a political tsunami was in the offing. People wanted change and relief from incumbent President Noynoy Aquino's administration which was perceived to be vindictive and insensitive.

A Barangay Chairman in Metro Manila finally filed his certificate of candidacy for President as the official candidate for President of PDP-Laban, [221] an accredited party to beat the deadline. Availing of the law on substitution, Rodrigo Duterte was later substituted as a candidate.

The timing was perfect! Binay was as good as politically dead because of the allegations of corruption. The true Grace Poe was unmasked as having betrayed her allegiance to her country by acquiring US citizenship and by later reacquiring Filipino citizenship showed opportunism to many, who also doubted her qualifications. It did not help that the Supreme Court's decision was less categorical and ambiguous as to leave the issue open for the future determination whether in a protest before the Presidential Electoral Tribunal in case she wins or further in the future when there might be another occasion that she would vie for the same position again.

---

[221] Partido Demokratiko Pilipino — Lakas ng Bayan Party — a left wing political party.

Meanwhile, there was a groundswell of support for Duterte who appeared to be a genuine choice among the presidential aspirants. The people saw in him a strong leader who was not afraid to challenge the traditional mindset like a swipe at the Pope and Catholicism; a tirade against the US; evoking the imperialist mantra; an independent foreign policy; a strong platform against the drug syndicates and crimes, and a clean government. In the past, all these outbursts of Duterte's would have spelt political doom but the people seemed to have finally shared a common sentiment on these issues.

Two weeks before the presidential election, the choice was unmistakable. Filipino voters in the Philippines and worldwide finally found an authentic leader.

Only few knew that he represented a generation that is the product of the spirit of the times that was made coherent by the cravings, musings and soul-searching among the students in our canteen in the university belt in the 1960s.

His election was a sign that the spirit of our student canteen had finally found a home in the heart of the mainstream Filipino constituency.

# 16
# EPILOGUE

*Forever and a Day. High up in the North in the land called Svithjod,* [222] *there stands a rock. It is one hundred miles high and one hundred miles wide. Once every thousand years, a little bird comes to this rock to sharpen its beak. When the rock has thus been worn away, then a single day of eternity will have gone by.*

—Hendrik Willem van Loon

The advent of Rodrigo Roa Duterte as the eloquent voice of the ideas of the canteen would not have been unexpected at all in 2016. And why?

Years had gone by, and the students of the canteen had finished their degrees. Most of them became lawyers. We met in a more expensive place that befits what we have achieved in life. But everyone admitted that we have not really graduated from the school of life that the canteen symbolised.

We asked ourselves the question: Did we succeed? Did we transcend?

I cannot help but compare an Ivy League school to our informal university, the canteen, which was also exclusive, but it was not in the sense of a privileged life but that we were all

---

[222] Mythical land in Sweden.

there by the common circumstance of being poor and socially disadvantaged. Yet there was heightened anxiety to shake off the evil of ignorance instead of indulging in self-pity.

Our individual thirst for knowledge and meaning was quenched by a collective sharing of our feelings and thoughts, the sum of which had the effect of making us more confident and prouder in ourselves. As we were not acting for and on behalf of anybody, it was the right place and time to learn to be free, to be brave and to be responsible.

Those who knew how to discriminate the chaff from the grain during the discussions and interactions made the right move at the right time, and there is also luck, common sense and courage and daring to act. Then how much you have learnt and how good you have become is continuously tested in random events and situations called experiences. We were metals in human form twisted and upgraded into useful material by the harsh necessities of life.

As there were many forms in what we became, there are many ways of looking at success.

The epiphany took place after more than fifty years in the wake of a deceased fellow student and a canteen fixture. There were impromptu eulogies, reminiscence of our lives together as students. They made light of the fact that the deceased had married at quite an old age of forty years old. The deceased was one of the best speakers in the university and in the canteen, but they insinuated that when it came to courtship, he was speechless.

We laughed endearingly.

When we were saying our goodbyes, one of the nephews of our deceased friend approached me and said:

"We were the reason he married late."

He was implying that his uncle was not gun-shy at all when it came to courtship.

I was curious.

He said: "I am now an engineer, and my siblings are also professionals. We are the children of his elder sister who helped him in his studies during your time. He did not marry until we finished our studies."

Here is a family liberated by knowledge and education from being poor not only in material things but in spirit as well. This was the deliverance we in the canteen had advocated and strived to achieve.

Then my classmate's nephew put his hands around me like a semi-embrace.

"My uncle was very proud of you! Right now, he is thanking you for what you have done to increase the retirees' monthly pension to two thousand pesos."

The memories of that political battle came back to me like a deluge. The proposal to increase the retirees' pension had been an emotional and furious national debate. When the Philippine legislature passed a law to increase the pension by two thousand pesos, the law was vetoed by then President Noynoy Aquino upon the advice of his finance secretary. It became Duterte's campaign promise to grant the pension increase once he became president.

It was easier said than done. Duterte was beleaguered by his own economic advisers, headed by the Secretary of Finance, with his Budget Secretary and National Economic Development Authority Secretary in agreement. As Chairman of the Social Security Commission, I gathered my own experts and scrutinised the actuarial report on the SSS fund's viability. It was so conservative that it had computed the actuarial life on an increase of contributions and investment income at only about 2% per annum. Conducting a simulation of the numbers based on merely a 6% increase per annum, the fears of the economic managers were more imagined than real because the actual numbers showed an annual increase of contributions and investment income at an average of 10% per annum, with plenty of room for improvement.

I presented the proposed increase in the meeting of the cabinet presided by President Duterte. In the debate among cabinet members that ended at about two o'clock in the morning, my proposal to increase the pension was approved. Fortunately, about two years after the increase was implemented, the actuarial life of the pension fund regained its pre-increase level.

I went back to my classmate's simple coffin and praised him for a job well done! I was referring to his own personal battles against poverty and ignorance. Perhaps, it was also for all the students in our canteen days to whom I owe the courage and inspiration to take the risk to improve the life of the retirees in their sunset days.

But before leaving I finally told him, silently: All is well that ends well.

During our early days in the canteen, there was no indicia at all of the worries in our private lives. Our individual problems were hidden from public view and scrutiny. That we did not cry on each other's shoulder to lament on our sad circumstances speaks of a positive outlook and inner strength mistaken for false pride.

Still, behind the facade of exuberance, we were still the 'Les Misérables' of Victor Hugo's novel whose day-to-day existence was too precarious. In a broader context, we were all sons of historical precedents consisting of foreign colonisation, exploitation, geopolitics, and even religious manipulation of the unlettered disguised as bringing civilisation, protection and God to an entire nation only to lay a nation into a wasteland of ignorance and servitude. Ordinarily, no being of sterling value would come out of these historical antecedents; instead, a pathetic figure of meekness, lack of pride and dependence is the logical outcome unless a personal change takes place.

But the canteen during our time provided us the place to talk, to contemplate, and to define the existential challenge to our personal lives. As we came face to face with our problems, the rhetorical jousts transcended the personal to what ills beset our community and the nation as a whole. We became aware of what we are and what and how we will be.

In that canteen, we were a microcosm of a nation finding its voice and identity, a quixotic attempt at our young age to dream of a new order. With education fostered by the university, it engineered an upheaval of mind and spirit unlike the multitude of Filipino revolutionaries at the end of the 19th century who were stirred emotionally by the abuses and death of Jose Rizal, the three martyred Filipino priests of Gomez, Burgos, and Zamora and the countless instances of the rich taking advantage of the poor, and then betrayal by their leaders.

It was not surprising that the stirrings of the peasant-revolutionaries, who mostly did not have the benefit of a critical examination of their lot which our canteen had offered, to bring down the Spanish colonialists and their resistance to American foray, would be hijacked by the better educated Filipinos and mestizos who did not have the historical antecedents or humble circumstance as we had. They wanted power for themselves to take the place of the colonial masters or share with the latter as vassals or alter egos. They are in fact resurrected by the graduates of Ivy League schools in our time who, with some exceptions, were devoid of cognisance or a sense of urgency.

If the peasant-revolutionaries, the foot soldiers of the revolution had been like us, the writings of our national hero, Rizal, could have resonated into an attitude of self-reliance, self-pride and independence of thought to the Filipino at large. Then the revolution of the last years of the nineteenth century and early years of the twentieth would not have been betrayed. Genuine nation-building would have started then and would have given us a hundred years' lead of development. We would not have been tossed aside by the interests of the powerful nations of the United States and Great Britain. There would not have been foreign military bases; Sabah could have been kept with its rich natural resources and minerals, and the West Philippine Sea[223] would truly be a Philippine territory or economic zone at our disposal, and Filipino workers would not have been treated as slaves overseas.

The ambience in that canteen offered a free and independent discussion of what ails the Filipino national psyche. It provided the momentum not only to the crucible to break the chains that enslaved us individually but also the crucible of a nation seeking its survival and a better future.

Our collective thoughts formed the genesis of a bold and independent Filipino mindset as shown among the Filipino leadership today.

---

[223] Which is now being claimed by China.

Having confronted the evil of ignorance, the new Filipino, the new man, is born.

I just hope it will not take this new man, like the little bird who sharpens its beak on the rock of Svithjod, a thousand years to level that mountain of ignorance which hides the morning sunlight of enlightenment.

> *That there should one man die ignorant*
> *who had capacity for knowledge,*
> *this I call tragedy.*
> — Thomas Carlyle (1795 – 1881)[224]

---

[224] British historian who wrote that "the history of the world is but the history of great men."